No Longer Two

A Christian guide for engagement and marriage

Brian and Barbara Edwards

A man shall leave his father and mother and be joined to his wife, and the two shall become one flesh. So then, they are no longer two but one flesh. Therefore what God has joined together, let not man separate.

Matthew 19:5-6

DayOne

First edition 1994
Revised edition 1999

British Library Cataloguing in Publication Data available
ISBN 1 903087 00 7

Published by Day One Publications
3 Epsom Business Park, Kiln Lane, Epsom, Surrey KT17 1JF.
01372 728 300 FAX 01372 722 400
e-mail address: sales@dayone.co.uk
web site: www.dayone.co.uk

Designed by Steve Devane and printed by Clifford Frost Ltd, Wimbledon SW19 2SE

Dedication

To the many couples at Hook Evangelical Church, Surbiton who helped to shape this guide.

Some comments from readers of the first edition

Thank you for your advice in *No Longer Two*. It brought up plenty of searching issues which stimulated lots of discussion
J&M / NEATH

No Longer Two has been a great help and blessing to us. The studies are very well put together and did much to strengthen our communication.
Thank you, **Y&D / MIDDLESEX**

My fiancée and I have just finished working our way through *No Longer Two*. I am writing to let you know how helpful we have found it. It has raised subjects that we might never have discussed. It has also given us Biblical thinking on subjects that we have already discussed.
Thanks for your helpful book, **PM / SURREY**

Over the last couple of months, we have been using *No Longer Two* with a young couple from our church. We are thrilled at the way that so many practical and spiritual issues have been brought to the forefront.
Thank you for your hard work, **DJM / CRAWLEY**

Contents

Preface to the second edition

On Monday November 16th 1998, Barbara entered from death into life. The previous two years had been a traumatic round of hospitalization, recovery, and a vain struggle to regain strength. During this time, our love grew deeper and the bonds stronger, which made my loss all the harder.

Among the hundreds of cards and letters I received following her death, most of which spoke warmly of the influence she had on so many lives, one particularly drew my attention as I thought of our relationship. Jim and Helen Sayers had worked with us as staff members, and they commented, 'For the past eleven years you have simply been "Brian and Barbara" to us, and *we really have thought of you both as one collective noun*! It is deeply strange to write to you on your own, simply because it makes us realise how much the life you had together was so supremely shared'.

I had never thought of that as a definition of marriage—'one collective noun'—but I know that Barbara would have endorsed it gladly.

When Barbara died, I lost my dearest friend, closest confidant, wisest counsellor, keenest critic, most loyal co-worker, greatest example, my only lover, and the best wife that any man could wish for. Barbara was my model of Proverbs 31. It is my prayer that all who use this book will be able to say the same of their partner, when for them the most beautiful of all relationships is finally broken only by death.

The response to the first edition of *No Longer Two* was often very moving for us both. Not infrequently we would be approached at the close of a meeting by a young couple who just wanted to say 'thank you' for the course. On one occasion, a car park attendant at an inter-church conference flagged us down, not to offer directions, but to tell us how far he and his fiancée had progressed through the book! The encouragement of so many church leaders to keep the book in print led to this new and revised edition.

Just forty-eight hours before the Lord called Barbara, we reached half-way in our revision. From there on, her notes and our many conversations on the subject have been my guide. I have been careful to make only those changes that I know Barbara would have agreed!

Brian Edwards
Surbiton, Surrey. July 1999

An important introduction

A notice hangs in the office of each Superintendent Registrar in England and Wales which reads:
'Marriage, according to the law of this country, is the union of one man with one woman voluntarily entered into for life to the exclusion of all others'.

This is the legal definition of marriage set down by Lord Penzance in 1866. Sadly, however, the law and the practice have become two very different things. With ever-increasing pressures upon the standards that are traditionally Christian, and with a growing percentage of Christian marriages breaking up, there is an urgent need to ensure that couples are adequately prepared for this great step into their future together.

This book has grown out of more than thirty years' experience of counselling couples before their marriage, during their marriage and sadly at times, when their marriage is all but destroyed. We have turned our experience into this short marriage preparation course. Many couples either gratefully enjoyed or graciously endured it whilst we fine-tuned it! Others have since used the course in their own counselling and we have also talked with couples after their first year of marriage to improve the value of the course still further.

Many books on this subject are intended to be read just as a book. It would not matter whether you read the book alone, or with your partner; whether you talked it through with anyone or not; or whether you read it in two days or two years. This book is different. As you will see from this introduction, it is a workbook above all else. We encourage you to discuss it with others and discourage you from reading it alone. We give you work, called 'assignments', at the beginning of each chapter. It is not an idle-hours reading book, but a disciplined study work book. This does not mean it is either hard or heavy, but it is demanding. However, preparing for a successful marriage is like most things in life, if your preparation does not cost you anything your achievement is probably not worth anything either.

This book is intended to lay some foundations. It will help you to think about some of the things that may have escaped your notice and, as far as possible, help you to prepare for the future. We try to cover every significant area of marriage. We start with engagement and discuss the joys and dangers of this important time. Even if you are already married, it is advisable to read this chapter because it begins to open up the vital subject of communication.

We then move on to study the biblical basis for marriage, and follow this with a discussion of problems with our in-laws, the different role of husband and wife, and the incompatibles that can so easily come between you. We try also to project ahead into some of the crises which may come into your life together, and how you will cope with them. Inevitably we must consider the subject of money and how you will organise your finances. We shall also discuss the delicate area of the intimate physical life of a husband and wife and help to prepare you for the possibility of starting a family.

There are two chapters on wedding-day preparations for those of you who are engaged. They are packed with practical help and suggestions that cover virtually every area of your preparations. If your wedding date is already fixed then we recommend that you go straight to these chapters.

Finally we have included a review one year into your marriage, or if you are already married one year from completing the first seven chapters. In fact to keep this guide close to hand and frequently dip into it may prove very helpful throughout those twelve months. Having it by you will act as a reminder that there is one chapter still to go. Don't read it before time—but don't forget it on time either!

Our approach has in mind those who follow Jesus Christ as their Lord and Saviour and therefore want to be obedient to his word, the Bible. However, since we believe the principles found in the Bible concerning marriage are universally relevant, we commend our course to all who want to find a strong foundation for their new relationship. With almost three out of five marriages contracted in the United Kingdom heading tragically for the divorce court, wisdom demands that you should take time to ensure that your marriage does not add to that tragedy.

Perhaps this book has been given to you and you are not Christians and do not go regularly to church. We would encourage you to buy a *New King James* Bible or a *New International Version* of the Bible to take with you into your married life. Do work at the Bible studies. There is an index at the front of every Bible that tells you where to find the books. You will be surprised at how relevant the Bible is today.

How to use this book

You will get the best out of this book if you follow the pattern we adopted in preparing the course. We strongly encourage you to find a mature Christian couple who are prepared to invest some time with you. Their experience and insights will prove to be a valuable help. They do not need to be an elderly couple, but should have some five years or so of marriage behind them; they should work through this course themselves and be in general agreement with it. Above all, they need to be a couple whom you respect, and whose marriage you know to be happy and secure. You will also need to be relaxed with them and willing to talk freely; naturally they will treat your discussions in total confidence. A pastor or elder and his wife would normally make an ideal team as helpers.

Sadly, in today's world we need to add a note of caution because what is intended to be a helpful course can end in tragedy. All counselling should be done as a foursome or if one partner wants to talk alone it must always be with the same sex; there should never be any opposite sex meetings alone. Don't give the devil a foothold.

You will need to plan a disciplined programme together. It is advisable to work through the book one chapter at a time, including its assignments and Bible studies, ideally over a period of not more than two weeks; this period will include an evening of discussion with the couple who are helping you. If you take much longer than this over each chapter, your minds will not be concentrated and you will lose the value of thinking through each section carefully.

Plan each fortnight like this: Set aside an hour or two to work on the assignment for each chapter; generally these require you to work on your own and not with your partner. Then plan an evening when you can work together on the Bible study for each chapter; make this unhurried so that there is time to let your conversation and discussion run on if you want it to. On the same evening read through the chapter in the book and discuss your assignments when it is appropriate to do so. Finally on another evening meet up with your helpers for an hour and a half. They will have read the chapter, and may even have attempted the assignments and Bible studies for themselves! Let them set the agenda for the evening and take you through the chapter. There is no need to read it again on this evening, but you can all stop off and discuss areas that are of particular importance to you.

We do not recommend using this course for group discussions; they are too threatening and few are willing to expose their fears and weaknesses to a group. If it is not possible to find experienced and wise helpers, then there is no reason why you should not just work through the book together; but you will need to be disciplined so that once started you work steadily through to the end.

Please don't be tempted to read the book and miss out the assignments and Bible studies. They are all carefully integrated into the chapters, and are planned to help you pray, talk and work together. As you read the chapters you will understand the real value of these assignments and Bible studies. It is essential also that you follow the directions and work on your own for the assignments when requested to do so; this will enable you to think on your own and without the pressure of giving the expected answer to your partner. All this is so important that we repeat the instructions before each assignment. The assignments and Bible studies come before each chapter so that if you disobey the rules you will have to make a conscious decision to do so! If you can't afford two books, you are free to photocopy the assignments so that you can work on them alone. Because the final chapter is intended as a review of your marriage twelve months on from finishing this book, it would be worth while keeping your assignment answers for future reference. Perhaps you should make a note in your next year's diary to remind you to work through the final chapter together.

The Bible translation we have worked from in this book is the *New King James* Bible, though occasionally we have indicated a preference for a translation from the *New International Version.*

We have deliberately not included 'model answers' to the questions, partly because in many instances there is no right or wrong answer, and partly because the chief purpose of the assignments and Bible studies is to encourage you in the habit of communicating and studying the Bible together. It will also help you to think deeply about your relationship. However, each chapter will contain some pointers to the studies you have completed.

This marriage preparation course is both practical and personal. At times it may make you feel uncomfortable as your partner learns of some of your deeper thoughts and attitudes. But always remember that honesty and openness are two of many keys to a successful marriage. Digging foundations is never light work, but the resulting construction can be very satisfying.

Although the book is especially valuable for engaged couples as a marriage preparation course, others have found it very useful in the early years of marriage. Please don't by-pass the first chapter if you are already married; there are many important principles laid down in chapter one.

Assignment for chapter one

This assignment should be completed on your own and without reference to your partner. Please do not discuss the questions or your answers until you read the first chapter together. Then discuss the assignment at the point in the chapter when you are recommended to do so.

Communication

1 Tick which of these subjects you and your partner have at any time discussed together; we do not mean subjects you have mentioned just in passing:

★ The Christian faith
★ How many children you would like
★ Your separate roles in the home
★ Your hobbies and sporting interests
★ Politics
★ The sexual side of your marriage
★ Your in-laws and parents
★ The style of house and furnishings
★ Family Prayers
★ The third world and its problems
★ The kind of food you prefer
★ Clothes
★ Your church and its members
★ Your finances and tithing
★ Your daily employment
★ The Bible
★ Abortion, and embryo research
★ Bringing up children
★ Gardening
★ Your love for each other
★ War and terrorism
★ The feminist movement
★ Books and television
★ Euthanasia
★ Your health
★ Current news items
★ Your relationship to the opposite sex other than your partner
★ Fears and phobias
★ Your views on alcohol
★ Styles of Christian worship
★ Spiritual gifts
★ Pets
★ Genetics and GM food

2 Now place a cross beside those subjects over which you are in strong disagreement.

To define love

3 Write down in one sentence your definition of the kind of love that qualifies for marriage.
4 When you don't feel a romantic love about your partner what is it that you still love about them?
5 What will you get out of marriage that you will not get if you remain single?
6 What are you hoping to bring to your marriage to make it work?

Bible Study for chapter one

You should work on this Bible study together. Find some unhurried time, perhaps the same evening that you plan to read the chapter together. ***It is important that you complete the Bible study before you read the chapter.***

Read 1 Corinthians 13.
Paul is writing to the church, but we can also apply this chapter to marriage.

1 In verses 1-3 Paul lists a number of things which in themselves are excellent, but his point is that they are no substitute for love. What good things can people put in the place of love in their marriage?

2 In verses 4-8 Paul lists sixteen phrases to describe true love. Work through these one by one, writing down just one word or short phrase to explain them. Use your own words rather than simply repeating Paul's.

3 Why do you think Paul claims that love is 'a more excellent way' (12:31) and is greater than faith and hope (13:13)?

Now we are engaged

HAVE YOU WORKED THROUGH THE ASSIGNMENT AND BIBLE STUDY?

In any construction work what you finally achieve will depend upon the plans you begin with and the secure foundations you lay. A marriage and a home are no exception.

When young people set out on a new career we send them to classes to train them, and we give them examinations to test their skill. They can switch track at any time if they don't like their chosen career, or if they fail in the tests. But when two people enter marriage, it is the second biggest decision of their lives. They will be in this career, sharing the same house and even the same bed, for possibly fifty years or more. There is no escape once the decision is made; for good or ill, whether they succeed or fail, the career has started and it lasts until one partner in 'the firm' dies. The only commitment greater than this, which every person has to make, is the decision whether or not to serve God—and the result of that decision lasts for eternity.

Sadly we rarely give much in the way of Christian counsel to a couple setting out on their great adventure. Unless they both come from a loving and consistent Christian home, they may have no idea what a happy and successful marriage really is. If one partner comes from a home where the marriage was a disaster, whilst the other comes from a caring home, the problems can be even greater. One has only a dream to hope for, whilst the other has a model to copy. The dream and the model may be very different. Stop here and spend six minutes talking together about your past: your childhood, your schooling, your home. Make a list of the differences between you. Without clear biblical counsel, the only information a couple may glean in preparation for their marriage comes from the world's opinions heard in the cheap jokes around the office and seen in the ever-falling standards of the media. We are all receiving advice—of one sort or the other.

Because marriage is a long-term commitment, the circumstances that you start out with will never be the same as those you finish with. And the changes in between are infinite. You can plan to get married quite easily, but you can never plan for the whole of your marriage. All you can do is to lay a solid foundation that will be firm enough to support all the adaptations and extensions that you will need to make in the years to come.

Every couple has blissful dreams of unbroken happiness. Those who also live in the world of reality know that it will not always be like this. Few couples are willing, or even able, to face the possibilities that may enter their life together.

Chapter 1

This book sets out to face not only the joys and privileges of marriage, of which there are many, but also the potentials for harm.

Your relationship in marriage must not be allowed to depend upon your present circumstances. Are you sure it will hold out, 'for better, for worse; for richer, for poorer; in sickness and in health'?

A personal testimony

To show you how circumstances can change in a marriage, we want to share with you a little of our own experience. There is nothing especially remarkable in our story, but it does illustrate the point we are trying to make.

During our secondary education we both enjoyed excellent health. Brian took part in hockey and cross-country running, and Barbara was games captain of her school. We completed our college training before we married, and then Brian taught in a grammar school and finally in a London comprehensive; at the same time he was assistant to the pastor of a large and growing evangelical church in south-east London. Barbara, meanwhile, worked in the office of a printing firm. Although generally healthy and strong, by the age of seventeen she had been diagnosed as having rheumatoid arthritis.

At the end of two years we moved to the full-time pastorate of an evangelical church in a London suburb. Brian studied, preached, visited, organized, served on a number of committees, edited Sunday school lesson helps, and began to write books. Barbara looked after the home and family, entertained visitors regularly, and acted as secretary, hostess, housewife and mother. At various times she taught in the Sunday school, and commenced a girls' Bible class, a young wives' fellowship, day-time playgroup, and a conference for pastors' wives.

Our time together and with the children was limited and we rarely took a day off. We entertained every Sunday and during the week. Financially things were not easy, and every month saw us counting the pennies carefully to see if we could get through to the end. We tramped the high street to get the best bargains, made our own Christmas and birthday presents whenever we could, holidayed with parents, and finally sold the car and took up cycling.

We both thrived on hard work, but our marriage didn't. It was not that it was falling apart; it just wasn't thriving. It was not growing into mature and deeper love. After a few years of this we began to talk about it. Well, to be accurate, Barbara began to talk about it and Brian slowly started to listen. We did some big re-shuffles in our programme and Brian shed some of his responsibilities. Our marriage mattered more than anything else.

At the same time the rheumatoid arthritis was grabbing at Barbara. Over a period of twelve years she spent sixteen weeks in hospital undergoing five major operations for orthopaedic surgery. Life began to change. Barbara was now more confined to the home; and was in daily pain with very little mobility and needing help with many ordinary tasks. Brian had to take on some new duties: washing, cooking and, worst of all, shopping! On the other hand, financially, for various reasons, things were much easier than they had ever been before. So, as one burden lifted another, and a very different one, fell heavily upon our marriage.

It wasn't easy. With a growing and active church and family, and increased demands upon our time, there had to be constant readjustments. There are stresses, pressures and tensions in every marriage, and ours was no exception. Our interests, hobbies, domestic duties, and Christian service all had to be thought through and changed. Carefulness in every area of our marriage was needed. Brian had to learn patience in a changing situation, and Barbara had to overcome the frustration of being dependent and less active. Only two things were constant: God's grace, which is all-sufficient, and our love for each other which matured and grew stronger with every passing year. Without these ingredients our marriage could never have survived; the pressures at times were immense. From games captain to a wheelchair is a hard route to take.

Eventually, Brian resigned the leadership of the church we had served for almost thirty years and we took up a new role. For two years we travelled widely throughout the United Kingdom visiting churches, speaking at conferences and attending committees. Our life was different, still busy but without the daily local church responsibilities; and at least we could do everything together. When this appointment came to an end we made plans for the future. But our plans were shattered within a few weeks. A major spinal operation left Barbara in a halo-jacket for three months and this was followed by one complication after another resulting in regular admissions to hospital. Barbara contracted the dreaded MRSA hospital bug and septicaemia followed. More than once there was little hope for her survival. Barbara was by now unable to do anything for herself and her life was reduced to resting in the morning and being transferred to her wheelchair at lunch-time to watch the world go by for the rest of the day. Once more it was all change. Brian's diary was dramatically reduced; a few hours work in the study each day was all he could manage. Daily visits by the community nurses and a constant focus on health care transformed our focus on life. But through all this we can honestly say that our love for each grew stronger and deeper.

The important point we want to make is that we could never have planned for all this before we were married. We could never have known it was all going to happen. These have been the adaptations and extensions built onto the foundation of our marriage, but because the foundation was deep and firm it could stand the changes.

A happy marriage comes from hard work. It doesn't come from books, magazines or videos, least of all from television programmes, dreams, wishful thinking or sweet words on the settee. Someone has called marriage: 'A total commitment of the total person for the total life'. A successful marriage is not chance, it is an achievement.

Why marriage?

That word commitment is not popular today. Because a generation stopped taking marriage seriously, their children see little value in it. Nearly three quarters of those in the 30s age-range believe that cohabitation, and having children without marriage, are acceptable. Most of them back their views by their practice. Marriage is seen as either avoidable – there is a better alternative, or expendable – it can easily be discarded. So, in the light of society's toleration for just living together and its acceptance of divorce as normal, why are you planning to get married?

First, marriage expresses the formation of a new family by separation from your present family. This is precisely the point made by God in Genesis 2:24, 'A man shall leave his father and mother and be joined to his wife, and they shall become one flesh'. Marriage is a public statement that a new family unit has begun.

Secondly, marriage is a commitment, not just to our partner but also to society, that we will care for each other from here on. The public act of marriage involves the community in its responsibility to hold each partner to the promises made. It enables society to say: 'We know you promised to care for each other, now keep your promise'. Co-habiting has no such security. Tragically, today's society has largely abandoned its responsibility to hold couples to their promises.

Charles Swindoll in *Strike the Original Match* compares marriage to home decorating. He claims:

It takes longer than you planned
It costs more than you expected
It is messier than you anticipated
It requires greater determination than you thought

We may add that it is also wonderfully satisfying.

Perhaps you are just engaged, or just thinking about marriage. So let's start by asking what the purpose of engagement is. You may already be a year or more into your marriage, but don't skip this next section. Keep reading, you never know what you may find!

What is the purpose of engagement?

You are in love! But what does that mean? Before you read any further, go back to your assignment and find out what you each answered to the section: **To define love.**

Many writers have struggled to find the meaning of love. For our purposes, we suggest that there are two types of love. First there is the ***romantic love*** which is the excitement, thrill and day-dreaming of two people engaged to be married. It won't last in quite the same form, but that doesn't really matter. Of course there needs to be excitement in every marriage, and throughout the marriage. But it isn't there all the time without interruption; and it changes from the heady, heart-throbbing, cloud-nine, thought-consuming love of a young couple who see stars whenever their loved-one coughs! This kind of love that often brings a couple together is not the kind of love that is needed to keep them together.

"Love offers security through sacrifice and does not merely grasp at pleasure without price"

Secondly there is what we call ***spiritual love***. By this we do not mean spiritual in the sense of religious, but spiritual in the sense of two minds meeting and two people merging into one in thought, interests, purpose and emotions. It is the love that longs for commitment more than for mere pleasure and is prepared to give as much as receive. This spiritual love is strong and durable. It is substantial, with its feet on the ground rather than its head in the clouds. It is mature and wise, not sloppy and sentimental. It is the love that offers security through sacrifice and does not merely grasp at pleasure without price.

You may have wondered: if we are in love, why bother with an engagement? Well, for a start, engagement focuses the mind on marriage. It is planning time. It is a commitment; the first step to the final commitment. During engagement you are learning to live within a commitment but without *the* commitment. This one may be broken—the next one must not.

Engagement time is also talking time. It is time to get to know one another with your eye on the future. Because of the engagement the relationship has a goal and therefore a purpose. You both know where you are going. There is no gentle skirting around the subject. All your friends and relatives know where you are going and that you are going there together. So engagement makes planning easier because everyone expects you to be planning. The commitment draws you closer. Engagement is an exciting time; a time when all your hopes and dreams begin to be shaped into reality! Couples just *drift* into living together, but you *plan* for marriage.

But there are dangers in engagement

Avoid an exclusive relationship. If you are in a youth group, now is not the time to be leaving. Keep your relationship in the group. Of course you will want to spend time together, but a sudden withdrawal into your own lives will hurt your friends, especially your single friends. Remember, you have something most of your single friends ache for. Don't add to their pain by leaving their company. If you abandon your friends and then the engagement doesn't work out, don't complain that you are now friendless. Attend all the meetings and invite some of your friends to share your happiness by sharing your company.

On the other hand ***keep your distance***. Avoid above everything kissing and hugging members of the opposite sex. You should always avoid this at all times, but it is even more important during engagement. We are well aware that this is a bit 'old fashioned' today, but the old ways are not always wrong. If your partner is constantly flirting, there are one of two reasons, and both should alarm you. Either they are trying to make you jealous, or they are not enjoying the relationship with you. Be sure of this: if a partner flirts now, the flirting will continue after you are married; if they hug and kiss others now, they will continue to do so later. Keep your distance. You show the greatest love and respect for the one you love by keeping 'touch' for that one person alone. Remember that the 'easy kiss and hug' syndrome can be very hurtful to the single people you flirt with; show them respect as well.

Avoid public loving. There are few things more degrading than to stumble across a couple in 'a close encounter' in a public place. It makes your love cheap. Physical expressions of love, like hugging and kissing, are private affairs. Is this old fashioned? Maybe, but it treats your relationship with respect and avoids offending others and hurting those who do not have a partner to love them. Think of others before you publicly express your love. Some find it embarrassing, others annoying, and others very painful.

Avoid going too far. One great danger is that you consider yourselves committed and therefore almost married. There are temptations to go all the way in making love. 'Why shouldn't we?' you may reason, 'We are committed, and we plan to marry anyway'. Almost all the media pressure goes in this direction—except that it generally doesn't bother with the marriage part or the consequences. Sadly, from this argument some Christians follow the world and persuade themselves that it is all right to live together before marriage. You should not because:

1 God says it is wrong. All sex outside of marriage is outside of God's plan. In 1 Corinthians 7:2-3 Paul actually says that marriage is necessary to avoid immorality. Hebrews 13:4 reminds us that 'Marriage is honourable among all

and the bed undefiled, but fornicators and adulterers God will judge'. The Bible is very clear on this issue.

2 It spoils the delights of anticipation. It is like a child finding their birthday present a few weeks beforehand; the delight of anticipation is ended. The real thing becomes a let down.

3 It carries with it the danger of a pregnancy and then a forced and hurried marriage without the joy of taking your time.

4 You may never marry. Engagement has an escape clause. If it doesn't work you can break it. But if you have already gone all the way, you have done something you can never undo. You have spoiled yourselves for the good thing to come.

5 To go too far will leave either or both of you with a conscience of guilt. And no marriage should begin in guilt.

6 Sex before marriage will frequently lead to problems within marriage.

So, to avoid going too far, avoid heavy petting. Never set out to show your love for one another in a way that deliberately stimulates your sex organs. Respect the wishes of your partner when they gently imply that you have gone far enough. Love involves respect. A partner who does not respect you during engagement will not respect you in marriage either.

Someone has wisely said that there are two rules in your love-making during engagement: No undressing, and no lying down together. If these become unbreakable rules, you can never go too far wrong.

Be wise in the time you spend together. The danger of the bed-sit is obvious. Avoid being alone together in a bed-sit; and if you must be there, set a curfew and keep to it. Never spend a night in the same house alone; never go on holiday together alone. We know this is against the common trend, but it is nevertheless sound advice. Make up a foursome or more, but never go alone. Those who want to obey God should not put themselves unnecessarily in the way of temptation. If you think any of this is unreasonably narrow, read together Matthew 5:29-30 and see how narrow Christ was!

Don't spoil your time of engagement by making it cheap.

You may be reading this, aware that you have already gone too far. You have been troubled about it and wonder whether things can ever be quite the same again. Remember that God is a forgiving Father. He has promised that if we honestly admit our sins and determine to keep to his rules in the future then he will: 'Forgive us our sins and purify us from all unrighteousness' (1 John 1:9). God means what he says. Take your Bible before you go any further and turn to the following passages, reading them slowly and thoughtfully together:

Psalm 51:1-6
Psalm 103:8-14
Isaiah 1:18-19; 43:25
1 John 1:7-10

It is always worth starting again with God. If this section presents a problem to you both, read the In Conversion booklet *Why shouldn't we?* also published by Day One Publications.

Motives for marriage

Have you ever stopped to ask yourself why you want to get married? You partly did this in the assignment: TO DEFINE LOVE (question 5). Here is a list of motives for marriage and the pressures that lead to those motives. As you read through them be very honest; ask how many fit you:

• To escape from home	The pressure of unhappiness.
• To find a companion	The pressure of loneliness.
• To enjoy sex	The pressure of lust.
• To appear normal	The pressure of society.
• To be loved	The pressure of insecurity.
• To love	The best motive of all.

If you have been honest, you will have found that some in the list were true of you before you reached the last one! They are not wrong and sinful; in fact they will all be present in your marriage motives to some degree. But if any of them, other than the last one, comes first in your priority, then think again; you have an unreliable basis for your marriage.

Look back at your assignment question 6. This will remind you that you need to concentrate on what you will give to your marriage rather than what you will get out of it.

A more excellent way

It is all too easy for a marriage to become like a grand historic mansion. We have all visited those splendid museums of luxury living. The furnishings are exquisite, the decorations lavish and the ornaments costly; you admire how neat and orderly everything is. Before long something very significant strikes you. People used to live here; once upon a time there was love and laughter. Now, everything is in place, but there is no life. It is a house, but not a home.

It is this difference that Paul has in mind in 1 Corinthians 13. Look back at your answer to the Bible Study question 1. Like the spiritual gifts Paul refers to at the end of chapter 12, your list consists of good things; they are the ornaments of a well-equipped marriage. But without the context of love they lose their value.

The second question in your study encouraged you to describe the kind of love that would turn the house into a home; a love that would bring life and warmth into your marriage. Paul calls love 'a more excellent way' because love is, above all, a relationship.

Communication

Communication is the key to success in any marriage. You must start talking together now. Turn to the first part of your assignment, the one called simply **Communication.** You may have wondered why we gave you such a long list of questions to check. Now you will find out. Exchange your paper and go through your partner's answers. Have you ticked and crossed the same things? The subjects were deliberately jumbled and there was no loading. The purpose is to discover whether you really are talking and communicating, or whether you just think you are. If you don't have many ticks down your list then you ought to start talking together and not just gazing into each others eyes. And if you have ten or more crosses, then your relationship is pretty explosive!

By communication we mean: 'Successfully imparting your opinions, hopes and fears to your partner, and hearing and understanding theirs also'. Communication is not just talking. If the other person isn't listening or doesn't understand what you say, there is no communication. There is no such thing as unsuccessful communication. You either communicate your message or you don't.

If you are constantly arguing together about different definitions or a misunderstanding about what the other meant, then you have no real communication. Sometimes you may feel like bursting out: 'If you would only listen to what I really say, you would understand what I am saying and not what you think I am saying!'.

There are three possibilities whenever you speak:

What you mean to say.

What you actually say.

What your partner hears you say.

Let's illustrate this. Suppose you said to your partner one day: 'If it was your mother's birthday we would invite her to dinner and give her some flowers'. That sounds innocent enough doesn't it? But here are those three possibilities:

You meant: 'Invite your mother to dinner, but we won't give her any flowers because it isn't her birthday'.

You actually said: 'We won't invite your mother to dinner or give her any flowers because it is not her birthday'.

Your partner heard you say: 'If it was *your* mother's birthday we would invite her to dinner and give her some flowers, but we won't for *my* mother'.

What a glorious row can develop over that little mess!

Communication is not merely talk. Here are some ways in which you can assist good communication in your home. But you will need to find the nearest equivalents in your engagement.

First, plan to talk. Set aside one meal-time every day when there will be no television, radio, newspapers or letters. You will just talk. Share the events of the day and swap news. This is especially important when children arrive in the home, so get into the habit right from the start. In our home we had two meals like this, at breakfast and the evening meal. When the boys were young, we always asked: 'Well, how did you get on at school today?'. In fact it is a golden rule in our home never to read a newspaper or magazine, and never to open mail, at the table. In your home don't let there be any reality in the old jokes about the husband buried behind the newspaper at the table.

Secondly, practice being honest and open. If you are worried about this now, it will become worse when you are married. If you believe you are not sharing openly your thoughts and fears together then perhaps you should begin by probing your partner a little here and there. If either of you is unwilling or unable to open up and share, then you do have a problem. But it can be overcome, and now is the time to overcome it. Perhaps your partner thinks you are not interested in their job or their worries; show that you are and never ridicule their views or opinions. It might appear exciting to be going out with that strong silent type of man, but it will be infuriating and frustrating when you are married to him.

Thirdly, learn to listen. Probably more than for any other reason our misunderstandings in communication arise simply because we do not listen to what the other person is saying. Here is a golden rule:

Listen with your mouth shut and talk with your ears open.

Don't be working out your opinions whilst your partner is telling you theirs; and don't cut in before they have had chance to finish, or begin. There is only one thing worse than the person who keeps finishing your sentences for you, and that is the one who won't let you start.

Proverbs 18:13 'He who answers a matter before he hears it, it is folly and shame to him'.

Fourthly, learn to look. When you are talking together, try to look at each other. Especially if the issue is delicate and you suspect there will be disagreement. Stop the washing up, crawl out from underneath the car, sit down opposite each other and look at one another. You have both already been practising the eye-talk that, even in a crowded room says, 'I love you'. That same eye-talk can communicate love even when you are disagreeing.

Fifthly, learn to touch. A squeeze of the hand or the arm, an arm around the shoulder, a quick kiss on the cheek, can communicate far more than a bunch of flowers or a box of chocolates—whatever the adverts may say.

Sixthly, congratulate and appreciate. Communication will be enhanced when you show your partner that you value them greatly. It isn't merely words and expressions of love that matter, but learn also to say 'thank you'. Many young wives long to hear a word of appreciation after the meal they have prepared disappears like magic; and the young DIY 'apprentice' will improve no end if he has an admiring wife to encourage him.

Never find yourself constantly ridiculing the efforts of your partner. The phrase: 'We hurt most those we love most' only reveals the sinful heart of us all. Never criticise your partner in public. You don't have to be blind to faults, but they are a private thing to be talked over together alone. If you down-grade your partner continually then you must not be surprised when eventually you are believed and you find yourself married to someone who has lost all self-respect. If, during engagement, your partner is always down-grading you, be alarmed! It means your partner feels very inferior and insecure and this is their defence—and it will not stop after marriage. Appreciation quickly dispels aggravation.

Finally. Avoid silent moods and nagging. They solve nothing.

Many young wives long to hear a word of appreciation after the meal they have prepared disappears like magic

Some ingredients for success

The ability to communicate is probably the most important single ingredient in your marriage, but it is not the only ingredient that matters. Take an honest look at yourself and each other, and see how far these are true:

Sensitivity. How far do you enter into each other's sorrows and joys? Are you caring and sympathetic, or does your partner walk away just when you need a little sympathy?

Stickability. If your partner can never settle to anything for long, whether it is a job, hobby or interest, then this may be a danger sign. Remember, your marriage is a long-term commitment.

Stability. Are you both emotionally and spiritually balanced? A partner who jumps in and out of extreme moods with unpredictable speed will be hard to live with for the next half century. Similarly, if your partner is easy prey to every new doctrine and experience that is current in Christian circles, this will provide a very unstable spiritual home in which to train your children.

Similarity. Of course two can become one even with widely diverse interests, but your social background, education, hobbies and your spiritual concern does matter. Your dissimilarities need be no barrier, but you must begin talking about them together now; and if you can't speak about them without a row or hurt feelings, then perhaps you should think again.

Stretchability (flexibility!). Marriage, as we have already indicated, is full of unexpected changes. Are you both able to adapt to changing circumstances and situations? Your reaction to changes at work or in your church will provide a guideline here.

Sense of humour. This is valuable for any marriage. We must be able to laugh at ourselves. There is nothing wrong with taking life and yourself seriously, but it can be a great strain living with someone who can never laugh at themselves.

As you have read through this chapter have you discovered anything in your relationship that has troubled you? This doesn't necessarily mean that you are incompatible, but it is a warning of potential trouble. Now is the time to get it sorted. Remember, engagement is an exciting time when all your hopes and dreams begin to be shaped into reality.

Bible study for chapter two

God's plan for our marriage

You should work on this Bible study together. Find some unhurried time, perhaps the same evening that you plan to read the chapter together. It is important that you complete the Bible study before you tackle the chapter. There is no other assignment with this chapter.

Read Genesis 2:18-25

1 How do you understand the words 'helper' and 'comparable' in v.18?

2 Why do you think God made Eve in the way he did? Why didn't he take a lump of mud, bring it to Adam and say: 'Look what I will do with this'?

3 How should we understand the word 'leave' in v.24?

4 What is meant by 'joined' in v.24?

5 Why does God draw our attention to the fact that the man and his wife 'were both naked... and were not ashamed' (v.25)?

Read 1 Corinthians 11:3

6 Can you draw a line diagram to illustrate the four-fold 'line of leadership' revealed in this verse?
Now, using dotted lines, add to your diagram the lines of fellowship.

7 How often do you plan to pray together when you are married?

God's plan for our marriage

HAVE YOU WORKED THROUGH THE BIBLE STUDY?

When God wanted to use a human experience to illustrate his relationship with his own special people, both in the Old Testament and in the New Testament, he chose marriage. Through Jeremiah God pleaded with unfaithful Israel to return to him, 'For I am married to you' (Jeremiah 3:14). In the last book of the Bible, the return of Christ is referred to like this, 'The marriage of the Lamb has come, and his wife has made herself ready' (Revelation 19:7).

God used marriage to describe his relationship with his own people because that was the best illustration of his bond. Genesis chapter 2 describes God's basic pattern for the relationship between a husband and wife. Have your Bible open at Genesis and look up the verses as they are mentioned.

It was a covenant of compatible companionship

The word love is not mentioned in Genesis chapter 2; but then, Adam was limited in the choice of his wife! According to God, marriage is a good thing (v.18). It is not the normal pattern to remain unmarried. The Old Testament has no word for 'bachelor' and the only word for a 'virgin' is an unmarried woman. This does not mean singleness is unnatural or odd, simply that it is not God's normal pattern.

God made woman as a helper; a companion as well as a lover. As a helper she would make up for his deficiencies. The two of them would make one strong unit. Adam was living in a world teeming with life and yet God said he was 'alone' (v.18); he needed a helper, a companion. She is indispensable to his well-being.

Turn to your Bible study assignment and look at your answer under question 1. Consider some of the ways in which Eve was a companion to Adam. In the first place she could help him to enjoy God's creation; God had made it all very good (1:31) and it was full of beauty. Perhaps as Adam gazed at the wonderful sights of creation and listened to the sounds around him he longed to share it all with someone. Perhaps he let out an exclamation of delight, only to find a stupid goat standing beside him! The animals just could not enter into Adam's appreciation of it all. But a woman could.

God had also told Adam that he was to rule over the creation (1:26) and to care for the garden in which the Lord had placed him (2:15). It was not hard work and toil at this time, but the woman could help him care for God's creation.

God also knew that later there would be problems and difficulties in the experience of life and two would be stronger to cope with crises than one. Besides, it was not good for man to be all on his own (2:18), something within him cried out for companionship. He needed Eve, not just to help him cope with all the problems that would come later, but to fill an emptiness in his life.

Finally, of course, Adam needed Eve to help him propagate the human race. God had given a command to all his creation that they should increase (1:22), but Adam had no one suitable for him; he needed someone to be specially made, so that he and she would be a perfect fit. Anything else would be unproductive and therefore unnatural. Nothing else fitted his needs like she did. She was a perfect match.

Adam was not created already married. God could have made Adam and Eve at the same time if he had wanted to; so it was a deliberate act by God to create Adam single. This way he would appreciate his partner all the more, because he knew what it was like not to have her.

When God said 'I will make him a helper comparable to him' (Genesis 3:18), the word 'comparable' (NIV 'suitable') literally means: 'corresponding to him'. She is man's counterpart. She is like him, but at the same time different from him. The idea is that of a compatible difference.

Discuss together the Bible study question 2.

God made Eve in the way he did so that Adam could never forget that she was special and had come from his own body. Nothing else in creation could substitute for her. Not even a man's parents can substitute for his wife. The way God made Eve reminded both of them that they could never be independent of each other. Adam knew this, and he said so (2:23). Immediately he could see that she was different, and in v.23 a new word is introduced into the Bible: In Hebrew man is *ish* and woman is *isha* She is 'female man'. That's what the word *isha* means.

It is popular today to play down the differences between men and women. In a publication for the Equal Opportunities Commission one writer comments, 'Apart from a few trifling differences of shape, males and females are essentially identical'! The rise of the feminist movement and the craze for female equality—sometimes even superiority—has made any discussion of those things that divide them more than unpopular; but our concern is to face the facts and distinguish the things that differ. In their book entitled *Brain Sex*, Anne Moir and David Jessel make the following thoughtful observation, 'Many women have been brought up to believe that they should be "as good as the next man", and in the process they have endured acute and unnecessary pain, frustration and disappointment… some women feel that they have failed. But they have only failed to be like men' (*Mandarin Paperbacks* 1991). We should explode the myth of sameness and celebrate difference.

The following paragraphs make some important points; think them through carefully before you react too negatively!

The most obvious distinction between men and women is **biological**, with the resulting physical differences. Since God created Adam and Eve naked, Adam must have noticed the difference! In fact the male and female bodies are a perfect fit for each other. This is one important reason why gay and lesbian relationships are so totally condemned in Scripture (see for example Leviticus 18:22, 20:13; 1 Corinthians 6:9); they are unnatural and defy God's perfect plan for men and women. Similarly the woman is perfectly made to carry and care for a baby. God planned her monthly menstrual cycle and it is a reminder of her great privilege in life. If ever the woman tries to be just like a man and imagine there is no significant difference, each month she has a reminder that God made her different! On the other hand, man is perfectly made for strenuous physical work and he doesn't have those monthly interruptions which can be inconvenient and tiring.

Men and women are also different **emotionally**. Women are generally more 'soft-hearted' and emotional. They cry more easily and are quickly upset by unkind words and actions. Men can be hard, even stony-hearted; they can be callous and indifferent to the pain and suffering of others. Actually they generally have a lower threshold of pain tolerance than women.

There is a **psychological** difference also. We are now beginning to tread on dangerous territory! Women are naturally more submissive and willing to be governed by men. They find it easier to be humble and peaceable, whereas men are more arrogant and assertive; generally wanting to be boss. Most women, contrary to what they are told to think today, want a strong leader to be their husband. All this is the natural pattern; it is not simply inbred by generations of prejudice. It was all part of how God made men and women. God made man first in order to be the leader. This is certainly Paul's argument in 1 Corinthians 11:8-10.

There are **spiritual** differences too. Women are very sensitive to the supernatural. Magic and mystery draw many women like a magnet. The traditional witch is a woman. And yet at the same time they are more easily frightened by all this. The woman is afraid, just because she believes it. Men are more concrete in their thinking, more 'here and now'; whereas women are more 'out there and then'. For him, seeing is believing. For her, believing is seeing. The woman thinks and worries about the future; that's why many mothers are uptight about the kind of world they are bringing their children into. Generally the woman is less this-worldly than the man; and that may be why there are more women on the mission field!

Now you may be reacting hard against all this; but stop and think for a moment. It could be that you are assuming it all adds up to the conclusion that one is inferior to the other. That is the reasoning of the world, but it is certainly not how God reasons. The Bible does not talk about superiority and inferiority, but compatibility. These are all compatible differences; but they are natural, not forced upon men and women by centuries of society's prejudices. God made woman 'similar'; and the word means: 'compatibly different'.

It was a covenant of cleaving companionship

Look again at your answers to the Bible Study questions 3 and 4.

The word 'cleaving' is a bit old-fashioned today and our translation therefore has the word 'joined'. If you look up the dictionary on the word 'cleave' you will find it has two meanings; and they mean the complete opposite of each other!

One definition comes to us via a Middle English verb 'to clove', which means to split something apart. The other definition also comes via a Middle English verb 'to cleave', which means to stick fast to something!

This is why the word 'cleave' is such a good word to describe a marriage. Look at Genesis 2:24. The man must cleave (split apart) from his mother and father and cleave (stick fast) to his wife. God's pattern is this: One man and one woman, sticking together through life and never split apart by any other man or woman—not even their parents. We will return to this subject in the next chapter because it is so vital; for now we need only establish the clear principles of leaving and cleaving.

One man and one woman, sticking together through life and never split apart by any other man or woman—not even their parents

It was a covenant of continuing companionship

There was to be no end to this relationship until death. Adam was never given the right to take a new model when he got tired of the first one. According to Christ, who preached a sermon on these verses, God joins the man and woman as husband and wife and no one should separate them (Matthew 19:6).

The subject of divorce forms no part of our discussion in this book. It is not on your agenda. The possibility may be there, but it is the impossibility that you are working towards. God's plan is simple and straightforward: one man and one woman united for life. That may be a long time, so firm and deep foundations are essential.

We are living in a society where it becomes progressively easier to opt out of marriage. Two writers committed themselves to the following advice in a book titled, *Divorce: How and When to let go,* 'Letting go of your marriage—if it is no longer good for you—can be the most successful thing you have ever done. Getting a divorce can be a problem-solving, growth-oriented step. It can be a personal triumph'. Today couples even talk about the 'experiment of marriage'. Of course the early years of a marriage may be stressful and sadly this is why many fail to survive, but we must resist the pressures of our modern society. A strong Bible base is the best way to start the resistance.

Sin spoiled everything

What did you make of question 5 in the Bible Study?

Adam and Eve had the ideal start that every young engaged couple must wish for. They had only each other to think about, no responsibilities, no distractions, and no in-laws! Added to this God placed them in a beautiful garden with warm sunshine, flowers and fruit, and no wild animals to alarm them. It was Tenerife all day and every day, but without the tourists. It was paradise.

Then sin spoiled everything. Look at the results of that first fall into disobedience recorded in Genesis 3.

It spoilt the gift of sex vs.7,10

Nakedness became an embarrassment to them (compare 2:25).

It spoilt their friendship with God v.8

God's presence now became a threat.

It spoilt their relationship together vs. 12-13

Compare with 2:23. But that was on his honeymoon when he was singing the praises of his new bride. Now the honeymoon is over and he speaks contemptuously of 'The woman whom you gave to be with me'.

It spoilt the woman's greatest joy v.16

Giving birth to her offspring was to be inevitably accompanied by pain for the woman. This is not true for any other part of God's creation.

It spoilt God's plan for harmony in the home v.17

Adam admitted that he allowed his wife to take charge (v.16) and that he took his orders from her. The woman failed on her first opportunity to take leadership. She led man straight into sin. 1 Timothy 2:13-14 is a commentary on this.

It spoilt their pleasure in work vs.17-19

Before the Fall, work was enjoyable and in harmony with creation (2:15), now man laboured with the natural order against him.

These results of sin in that first marriage affected almost all the areas of potential strife in any marriage: sex, worship, respect, suffering, leadership and work.

Marriage was the first human relationship to be spoiled by sin. When Satan looked around to spoil God's creation, the first target he aimed at was the marriage of Adam and Eve. **Your** marriage will be under attack also. This is because every couple today inherits not only the pattern of Genesis 2 but the problem of Genesis 3. Sadly, you will be marrying into Genesis 3 and not Genesis 2. You are both fallen sinners.

In the Old Testament God shows us how it all went wrong. Now we will see how it can all be put right.

Restoring the pattern

1 Corinthians 11:3 presents us with God's order of leadership: 'I want you to know that the head of every man is Christ, the head of woman is man, and the head of Christ is God'. This passage is not just about worship or head covering, it is God's blueprint for leadership.

Because the woman could not be trusted to accept her husband's leadership, God reminds her of her obligation. When Eve usurped Adam's role, she led him into sin; as a result she must learn that he will rule over her (Gen.3:16). In any community there must be order and leadership. This is true of heaven, and it needs to be true on earth also: internationally, nationally, socially, industrially, in the church, and in the family.

Many theologians have discussed the exact meaning of the word 'head' in 1 Corinthians 11:3 and Ephesians 5:23. Some believe it simply refers to source or origin and has no reference to authority and submission; in other words as Eve was taken from Adam's side (Genesis 2:21) so man is the source of woman. However, careful study by the American scholar Wayne Grudem shows clearly that the use of the word, both in the New Testament and in the Greek translation of the Old Testament, demands the meaning of authority.

In 1 Timothy 2:13,14 Paul makes it clear that the reason the woman must not have authority over a man in the church is two-fold: Adam was created first, and Eve was deceived first. Therefore the role of man's authority was established before the Fall.

It is never adequate to make diagrams of spiritual truth, and you may have played around with various shapes and lines before you finally decided upon your answer to the Bible study question 6. The chances are that you ended up with a vertical line, placing God at the top and the woman at the bottom; if you were a little more careful you may have produced a triangle, because that is often used to describe the marriage. But none of these adequately takes into account all that our verse contains. A better result is to use a square (see the diagram).

The use of the square emphasises that God and Christ are equal, yet Christ submitted to his father in the leadership line. In the same way the husband and wife are equal, yet the wife submits to her husband's lead-

ership. Leadership does not imply superiority, and submission does not imply inferiority. There is a dignity and value in submission. We have a clear pattern to follow.

That is the leadership line, or the authority line. But of course both the man and woman can individually communicate with the Father and the Son. So a dotted line called the fellowship line can be added (see the diagram).

It is important to understand the difference between leadership and fellowship. To find out how this leadership works, we must turn to two other passages in the New Testament.

Now read **1 Peter 3:1-7** together.

There probably is significance in the fact that Peter addresses six verses to the wife and one to the husband! The pressure to reverse God's order has, historically, almost always come from women.

Before we look at this word 'submissive', you should notice something very important that Peter slips into verse 1 and some translators have slipped out. What Peter actually says is: 'Wives...be submissive to **your own** husbands'. You will find the same phrase in 1 Corinthians 7:2 as well.

Peter wasn't making an issue, but he means what he says. He warns against giving the affection, loyalty, faithfulness and submission, that belongs to a marriage, to any one else other than 'your own husband'. Peter seems to have had a particular problem in mind as the rest of the verse shows. Some women were already married to unconverted husbands and their danger was to transfer their submission from their own husband to a wise leader in the church—someone else's husband. The motives may have been good, but the result could be disastrous. 'Hands off', says Peter, 'Keep to your own husband'. We must never lose sight of that; it is vital. Your husband is your ultimate leader on earth. Your own husband, and no one else's.

Now to the word 'submit'. We will return to the practical application of 'submission' in chapter 4, so at this point we need only establish the principle. The same word is used in 1 Peter 2:13, and in Ephesians 5:21,22,24. Look at the pattern there: 'As the church is subject to Christ'. That is not slavery and fear. Jesus called us his friends (John 15:15). And in that same verse he tells us why. Unlike the slave owner who demands unthinking obedience to orders, our Lord shares with us and expects us to follow him out of love. A wife is the best friend any husband can have. Of course she is much more than this, but she submits to his leadership just as the church gladly submits to the leadership of Christ.

This is exactly where Eve went wrong; and many of her daughters after her. Some wives boast that they really run the show. Pressurised by the thinking of the feminists in today's world, they find it hard to recognise that the husband should be the leader. Subtly, like Eve, she calls the tune, and when she wants his opinion she gives it to him. A hen-pecked husband, and a woman who wears the trousers in the house, are both unnatural and unbiblical. Few boss-women respect their husbands. That should speak for itself.

The word 'submit' means literally 'to arrange under'. That's why our diagram of 1 Corinthians 11:3 was the shape of a square. Look at it again. It means that the wife must take the subordinate position; accepting that 'he shall rule over you' (Genesis 3:16). It means admitting right from the outset that he is in charge. Never mind all the problems that rush into your head; we can deal with these later. Peter says: 'Do not give way to fear' (1 Peter 3:6 NIV), and that is sound advice. Don't start worrying, get the foundations laid first and you can discuss the colour of the curtains later!

A wife is the best friend any husband can have

Generally, Sarah got her leadership sorted out; you could tell that by the respectful way she referred to her husband (1 Peter 3:6). There is an important lesson there too. How we speak to our partner tells everyone what we think about them. On just one occasion Sarah was tempted to take on the roll of Eve, and with almost as disastrous consequences. If you read the first six verses of Genesis 16 you will see what we mean.

Now for the husband!

'Dwell with them with understanding' is how Peter starts (1 Peter 3:7). The words literally mean: 'Live with your wife according to knowledge'. You have a life-time to get to know your wife, and you will need it! Learn to understand her fears and anxieties, her moods (what puts her in them and what gets her out of them) and her needs. You are her pastor as well as her leader. Most wives want to submit to a husband they respect—and respect the husband they submit to.

Your wife is a delicate treasure, she is the 'weaker vessel' (v.7). If you batter and bruise her emotionally, spiritually, mentally or physically, she will be no use at all; but if you care for her lovingly she will respect you. Some men spend more time trying to understand their car than trying to understand their wife. That is ridiculous. You can sell your car and buy a new one!

Having worked hard to understand your wife, you then live according to what you learn about her. That's what it means to live with her 'with understanding'. Live as you know she would like you to live.

Just in case the husband thinks he can get away with some quick psycho-analysis and a bunch of flowers, the Bible hammers home in another place:

'Husbands, love your wives'. 'Oh, but I do', you respond, 'that's why I want to marry her'. Then the Bible adds: 'Just as Christ also loved the Church and gave himself for it' (Ephesians 5:25). That total self-sacrificing love explodes our smug self-satisfaction.

Love is the only sure basis for marriage, and it is addressed to the husband primarily. The reason for this is that most women want to marry a man they love, but men are often prepared to marry a woman they want to use as a mistress.

Love like Christ loved, says Paul in Ephesians 5, or don't get married at all
Love her into being the best and most perfect wife ever (Ephesians v.27)
Love her like you love your own body (v.28)
Love her like you love yourself (v.33)

Any woman who is loved like this has no more fear submitting to her husband than the Christian has in submitting to Christ. We know that Christ has only the best in mind for us. In the same way the wife who experiences this love from her husband knows that he always has her best interests in mind.

Back to 1 Peter 3:7. The husband is to treat his wife with 'honour'. The word means value. She is your most priceless possession, as well as your most expensive!

'Who can find a virtuous wife? For her worth is far above rubies' (Proverbs 31:10).

In 1 Peter 3:7 Peter gives three reasons why the husband should give consideration and honour to his wife:

First, she is the weaker partner. Handle her with care.

Secondly, she is your sister in Christ. You are therefore heirs together of the same gracious gift of eternal life.

Thirdly, she is your partner in prayer. Bad relationships in the home block up the path of prayer.

These rules bring freedom. Marriage is like a locomotive. All the time it keeps to the lines it will run along smoothly, but if it once leaves the track it will inevitably get bogged down.

The Bible has the best understanding found anywhere concerning the relationship between a husband and wife. It alone tells us where the relationship went wrong, and how it can be put right. Perhaps you are both aware that neither of you has submitted fully to the rule of Christ and his word, and that's why our constant emphasis upon what the Bible says seems strange. Now is the time to take Christ seriously and to recognise that he died for you in order to take away your sin, place you under his entirely new management, and give you a strong relationship with each other for the future.

Family prayers

This is where the closest bond between a husband and wife is made. Do you remember that at the close of Peter's instructions to husbands and wives he adds the words: 'So that nothing will hinder your prayers' (1 Peter 3:7 NIV)? This is the reason why the husband should live with his wife according to his understanding of her, considerately and respectfully. What mattered to Peter more than anything else was that the family prayer life should not be hindered.

When Peter speaks of 'your prayers' both words are plural. He is addressing himself to both husband and wife, and he has in mind all their prayer life: together, alone, and with others. And the word 'hindered' is used of blocking up a road to slow down the advance of others. Paul uses the same word to the Christians in Galatia. He has been complaining about their doctrinal backsliding and asks them 'you ran well. Who hindered you from obeying the truth?' (Galatians 5:7). Or, as another translation puts it: 'Who blocked up the road along which you were travelling so well?'

Some young couples start on this road of praying together...but then something happens to spoil it.

Some young couples start on this road of praying together and go at it very well; but then something happens to spoil it. Over the many years that we have been talking to Christian couples about marriage, all of them have agreed that this is a must for their life together; almost all of them have started to pray on the very first night of their new life, but many have totally failed within a few months. Sometimes ten or more years later they come back and ask for help in starting off again.

Of all the subjects we discuss this is probably the most important. Love starts here, communication starts here, and disagreements can be ended here at the place of prayer.

What do we mean by 'family prayers'? First of all, don't attempt too much. In your enthusiasm now, you may determine to set aside an hour for Bible study together each day. We doubt whether you will keep it up! Aim at what you can reach. Find a convenient time each day when you can spend just five or seven minutes together reading the Bible and praying. This should become a daily habit and when the first baby arrives he or she joins in as well. In this way family prayers has developed naturally. It is a good thing for a child to know that from birth it was surrounded by prayer and that it cannot remember a day when the family did not pray together. Visitors to the home should be included. The husband is the head of the home and can courteously invite relatives or friends to join in family prayers.

We suggest that you simply read a passage from the Bible, perhaps with a commentary to accompany it if you find this helpful, and then pray round. Naturally you will be sensitive to unconverted visitors, and you will not embarrass them. If they are present it may be wiser for only the husband to pray. But when you are together as a family you all pray; including the youngest child who is willing to offer a simple prayer. But make sure even the new baby is with you so that from the earliest days they are breathing the atmosphere of prayer.

The best way to ensure that you keep to this is to make it a daily rule in your home. Preferably at a set time every day. This will probably be at the meal you spend together as a family communicating. It doesn't matter whether it is breakfast or tea. We are aware of the difficulties when men have to leave home early and arrive back late, but find a way if you possibly can. At least on the weekend you should have no excuse.

All this is the irreducible minimum. Anything less is nothing. But it will open up whole new lines of communication and will pay rich dividends in later years.

In addition to this you will give thanks before each meal. Take it in turns to do so, but it should always be the husband who asks a member of the family to give thanks, and not the wife. It is the reverse of the biblical pattern for the wife to be heard asking, especially when there are visitors in the home, 'Will you say grace, dear?' This regular and yet brief time of prayer before each meal provides a natural opportunity to bring before God any other immediate items for praise and prayer. In this way prayer becomes a natural and regular part of your home life.

Finally, you will want to close each day together in prayer. Some couples like to have a time of Bible study at the close of each day, but again, don't attempt too much. You may prefer to read from a devotional book or from a book of daily readings. There are many such books available from reliable Christian publishers. Don't be afraid to change your pattern regularly to keep your reading fresh. Close the day in prayer together whatever you do. Perhaps you need to turn back to the last question in the Bible Study and correct your answer!

Why is this matter of family prayers so important?

First, because there is no greater cure for family rows and disagreements. If you always pray before you go to sleep you will never disobey the apostle's command: 'Do not let the sun go down on your wrath' (Ephesians 4:26). Or, as J.B.Phillips paraphrased it, 'Don't go to bed angry'.

Secondly, because there is no better way to lay a foundation for the spiritual life of the family. Pray regularly and you can pray at any time without embarrassment. If you pray regularly as a family you will talk often as a family about the things of Christ. When something good, or bad, happens, you can stop at once and turn it into prayer. It will become natural to pause before you set off on a long journey and pray before you belt up!

Thirdly, because there is no more valuable way to instruct the children in the Christian faith than regular family prayers. Christ will be the centre of your home. He will be seen to be the centre, not by the text-card hanging in the hallway, but in your daily family prayers. In our counselling of young people from Christian homes one of the greatest sorrows has been the large number who have never prayed with their parents in a regular and systematic way. This is not merely a tragedy, it is a disaster.

The importance of praying together regularly, even during engagement, is that you will learn to communicate spiritually with each other and then all other communication will be easier. The first baby will arrive into a home with parents who have surrounded it with prayer. When your children reach their teenage years you will be able to turn to the Scriptures and pray with them in a natural way. But you must start now in order to establish a consistent life pattern. Children, and teenagers particularly, are quick to notice any inconsistency in the home.

The importance of praying together regularly... is that you will learn to communicate spiritually with each other

If you are engaged to be married, pray together now. Don't think it will be easier when you are married. If you cannot pray now you will not pray then.

The wife's pastor

The husband should not forget that he is the guardian of his wife's spiritual welfare. Just as he should have a time of personal worship each day on his own, so it is the wise husband who enquires from time to time to ensure that his wife has the same. It is so easy for her to be harassed by housework and shopping and when the children arrive there seems to be no free time in the day at all. But every Christian wife must set aside some time, perhaps with her morning coffee or whenever it suits her best, to be alone and quiet with God. Again, it is not the length of time that matters. Five minutes with God is worth more that twenty-five minutes merely going through the motions of a time of prayer.

The husband as spiritual guardian of the home has a responsibility also to ensure that his wife is regular in attending worship, ministry and fellowship at church. When there is a young family, a consistent pattern of alternating is important: the whole family out on a Sunday morning, the husband and wife alternating on Sunday evening and at the mid-week meeting. Always talk together and share the service when you get home. Not in a grumbling spirit, but in a positive way. This includes the notices also. Many wives are never told the important information that was shared at the prayer meeting, because the husband didn't bother to pass it on; and anyway she didn't ask. When one partner is forced to stay at home through illness or domestic responsibilities, the other must take up the duty of sharing the news and, above all, the outline of the sermon. That should guarantee at least one sermon you listen to carefully!

A cord of three strands

By no means have we exhausted the Bible on the subject of husbands and wives, but we have laid a necessary foundation. Leadership, submission and love are the hallmarks of the Christian home. A tall order for just two people—and sinful people at that. But God's pattern is both natural and right. It gives dignity and confidence to the husband, and dignity and security to the wife. If he is to be the head of the home, she is certainly better equipped to be its heart.

Although the Bible lays the responsibility for spiritual leadership upon the husband, marriage is, however, intended for **mutual** encouragement. If one partner is spiritually or emotionally 'down' it is the privilege and responsibility of the other partner to lift them up. This is one reason why regular family prayers is so important; it is the way by which you keep in touch with each other spiritually. If either partner refuses to pray or declines to read the Bible then it is time to ask questions. The preacher in Ecclesiastes is quite right, 'Two are better than one because they have a good reward for their labour. For if they fall, one will lift up his companion' (4:9-10). Surely Job knew the meaning of this as he looked back to the years of his family life, 'When God's intimate friendship blessed my house, when the Almighty was still with me and my children were around me'. (Job 29:4-5 NIV).

Two into one can go. However, the best marriage is not just two into one, but three into one. A perfect blending of friendship and submission to one another and to Christ. Ecclesiastes 4:12 is a lovely text for any marriage: 'A threefold cord is not quickly broken'. In fact you will find verses 9-12 good to read. But make sure that third strand is Christ—and Christ alone.

Assignment for chapter three

The family on the fringe: Parents and in-laws

This assignment should be completed on your own and without reference to your partner. Please do not discuss the questions or your answers until you read the chapter together. Then discuss the assignment at the point in the chapter when you are recommended to do so.

1 How old were you when you:
Started to buy your own clothes?
Organised your own holidays?
Planned your own finances?
2 How often do you expect to phone your parents when you are married?
3 How often will you visit your parents-in-law?
4 Where do you expect to spend your first Christmas together as husband and wife?
5 If one of your parents died within the first two years of your marriage, would you offer the surviving partner a home with you:
Without hesitation?
Only after careful thought?
Under no circumstances?
6 Do you respect and love your parents?
7 Do you respect and love your in-laws?
8 What will you especially miss about your parents' home when you get married?
9 What qualities of your parents' marriage would you most like to be true of yours?
10 Do you expect your partner to reflect the things you valued most in your own mother or father?

Lowering the drawbridge

11 How would you define the difference between a house and a home?
12 The Bible commands us to be 'hospitable'. How would you define that word?
13 What action would you take if family or friends arrived on your doorstep on Sunday afternoon and clearly expected to stay for the evening?
14 Planning your time is very important. Can you list in order of priority the six most important ingredients in your week, excluding your daily employment, eating and sleeping!

Bible study for chapter three

The family on the fringe

You should work on this Bible study together. Find some unhurried time. ***It is important that you complete the Bible study before you read the chapter.***

Parents and in-laws

There are very few examples in the Bible of the relationship between children and their parents-in-law, but here are two:

1 Exodus 18 is the story of Moses and his father-in-law Jethro. As a Midianite priest Jethro was unlikely to have been of the same faith as Moses. Was Moses right in his response recorded in v.24?

2 The relationship between Ruth and her mother-in-law was one of sincere love and loyalty. Notice especially Ruth 1:16 and 3:16. The fact that Ruth had such a relationship with Naomi in her young widowhood is strong evidence that she had such a relationship before her husband died.

Can we learn any lessons from these two stories?

Lowering the drawbridge

Read together Romans 12:13, Hebrews 13:2, 1 Peter 4:9-11

3 From these verses the New Testament underlines the importance of hospitality. It is a command to the Christian home, not an option. What different forms of entertaining would come under the title 'hospitality'?

4 List the categories of people you propose to entertain in your home and how often you will give hospitality.

5 What do you think are the advantages of hospitality?

6 Here is a rewarding study in the example of Aquila and Priscilla. Read the following verses and notice how their home was at various times: a guest house, a school of theology, and a place of Christian worship.

Acts 18:1-2, 26; Romans 16:3; 1 Corinthians 16:19

The family on the fringe

HAVE YOU WORKED THROUGH THE BIBLE STUDY?

Marriage is not just about uniting with your partner, it is also about leaving your family. We have looked together at Genesis 2:24 in our last chapter: 'Therefore a man shall leave his father and mother and be joined to his wife, and they shall become one flesh'. This is one of the most crucial verses in the whole marriage programme. Jesus underlines it in his teaching recorded in Matthew 19:4-6. Engagement is the beginning of the leaving and cleaving. Marriage is severing the umbilical cord and a failure to do so will create unbiblical chaos.

We appreciate that many young people preparing for marriage actually left home some years before, either to follow a course of study or to set up on their own. Even so, you must be sensitive to the fact that some parents will find this final break hard to accept. For this reason the following advice, which is directed particularly towards those who are still living at home, is relevant also for those who have already 'moved out'.

It should not be too difficult for you to begin to leave your families. You are deeply in love and you want to spend as much time as possible together. However, do be sensitive to your parents who may just be getting used to the idea of losing you. Whether or not you have already left home you should be discussing now how much time you spend with your families. You are both about to leave home physically, but you must leave home in your mind as well as your body.

As you discuss your assignment answers you may be surprised at your partner's responses; you may even find yourself disagreeing with them. Discuss, but don't argue. This is a difficult area, and perhaps you have not really talked it through before. But you must talk about it now because this subject has caused many problems in marriages. This is the reason for the traditional jokes about the 'in-laws'.

Turn to the assignment question 1. Your answers may reveal that one or other of you has not yet begun to break away from the strong influence of parents and is still heavily reliant on them for even some basic and simple decisions. You need to talk over these areas and work out a way of becoming more independent.

When you get married, how often will you phone your parents? The answer should be: 'Not too often.' A mother who expects a call every day from her son or daughter is demanding too much. In order to make the break, a weekly call to or from your parents is quite sufficient.

How often should you visit? Again, not too often. Visits should generally be by arrangement. The mother who calls in every day is a menace! Beware of the parent who may be dependant upon you. This can very easily happen if one parent is left. Great sensitivity is required on your part because you do not want to be hurtful, but parents must learn that God's plans are best. Just as you are discovering a new future, so they must.

When you are married your vocabulary must change. 'Home' is where you are now. You never go 'home' to mum and dad; and you never go 'home' for holidays. It will be hard for you to drop this vocabulary and it may drag on for years, especially if your parents are still living in the house in which you grew up; but work at it because it is important.

You have new obligations when you are married. Your parents don't have to be informed of your plans and decisions. Of course it is good to keep them in touch because they will still be concerned about you. But when you are married your responsibility for decision-making is to each other, not your parents.

Where you will spend your first and subsequent Christmas and holidays is, of course, a matter of personal preference and sometimes financial necessity. Don't forget to spread things evenly among the in-laws. There is no reason why you should not invite parents to join you at Christmas.

If you have problems with interfering parents, you must be firm. The partner whose parents are causing the trouble must talk kindly but frankly and make it clear that you do want to live your own lives. It is better to risk upsetting your parents right at the start than to let the problem fester and spoil your marriage for years to come. Deal with the issue quickly, and parents who cannot let go will soon get the message.

Be on your guard against brothers and sisters, aunts and uncles, even grandparents, upon whom you may be too dependent, or who may be too dependent upon you. If they come to stay for a while, make sure they never stay too long.

What did you make of question 5 in your assignment? It is unwise to promise parents that there will always be a home for them with you if they need it. You do not know what your circumstances will be and you may not be able to keep that promise. You can promise to care for your parents always, without promising a home with you. Many families have been broken up by a parent coming to live with them. Even when parents have been successfully accommodated in the home, we have had a number of friends tell us of the tensions and pressures it has put on them and their children. On the other hand, it is not always easy for the parents themselves to settle in, especially in a home where teenagers are loudly in residence! Of course this doesn't mean that it is wrong for elderly parents to live with you; sometimes it becomes a really enjoyable experience, but it simply means that you will think long and hard before an offer is made; and then only if both of you are in full agreement.

Cultural and financial implications have to be considered, but you must remember the fifth commandment to honour your parents, and you must respect and treat them how you would like your children to treat you when your turn arrives. There are many good warden-controlled flats that allow elderly folk to still live independent lives. But regular visits, outings and even holidays in your home, will be greatly appreciated.

Perhaps one or other of you find a serious relationship problem with in-laws. Whose fault is that? Strangely it is not infrequently the father who is unwilling to let his daughter go. The evidence of this will be felt as soon as serious courting begins. Some fathers resent any man who rivals his influence over a daughter and the young fellow soon discovers a frosty welcome in the prospective in-laws' home. You both need to recognise and admit this and then discuss your response. An aggressive self-assertiveness will only make things worse. Aim to win over the protective father by working hard for a good relationship, and be prepared to invest some time for this. If you happen to share the same interests or hobbies, exploit it!

Show respect, loyalty and appreciation to your mother-in-law and you will generally win a friend

It is also true that some mothers are over-protective for their son. After twenty years of cooking, caring, mending, bed-making and a thousand other motherly duties, no girl will be quite good enough to care for the product of her investment! A daughter-in-law must accept this humbly and not try to outdo the mother-in-law. You can't match twenty years in as many months. Be patient. Show respect, loyalty and appreciation to your mother-in-law and you will generally win a friend.

Never quote your parents to defeat your partner in an argument; that is the best way to end a marriage.

Never criticise your partner to your parents or in-laws; that only makes for family feuds. Remember that if you keep on, in front of his parents, about how lazy, untidy and inept he is, you are criticising the very people who perhaps allowed him to become like that.

Never critically discuss one set of parents in front of the others; that is dynamite.

In talking with many couples we find that it is the wedding preparations that often bring these problems to a head. Parents who will not let go will demand the right to decide every detail of the wedding day. You must stand together and resist over-much interference in what is, after all, your day. We will have more to say about this in chapters eight and nine which are designed especially for those who are planning their wedding day.

Look back in longing?

By now you should be appreciating how important to your marriage is 'the family on the fringe'. Every marriage is the joining of six people; half a dozen genes from each parent makes you. It has been said that everyone carries their parents around inside.

You will have noticed there is not much in the Bible that speaks about our relationships with in-laws. Partly this is due to the fact that in Bible times, little difference was made between in-laws and parents in the honour we should give them. But your Bible study together pointed you to two positive in-law relationships. Moses was not too proud or too independent to ignore the wisdom of his father-in-law Jethro. The strong bond between Naomi and Ruth provides an excellent example of a loving mother-in-law/daughter-in-law relationship.

Discuss your assignment questions 6-7. You will have learnt many things from observing your parents over the years; and your family traditions will inevitably differ from those of your partner's family. For this reason you need to talk through these traditions. For example, if your father-in-law always put out the rubbish, but in your own home it was mother who did it, don't wait until you are knee deep in trash before you begin talking about the problem! If your family always bought a real Christmas tree each year, but your partner's home settled for an artificial one, then accept the fact that one of you will have to break with years of tradition. These are trivial issues compared to the ones that may come up in your discussion!

Of all your assignment questions for this chapter, 8-10 were possibly the most deceptive. Whichever way you answered, you are both right and wrong! There is nothing wrong with your admiration and enjoyment of aspects of your parents' marriage and home; in fact it is both natural and right if you have experienced a happy home life. So to identify some of the best areas is a positive thing to do. However, the danger zone is when you try to implant these into your own marriage. The best things from your parents' marriage and home are the plus factors that you may wish to bring to your own marriage, but be sure that your own partner agrees that they really are positives.

Of course the respect that your father always showed towards your mother is a plus factor to copy into any marriage, but your admiration of the way your mother pandered to your father may not be appreciated by your own partner! You must learn to distinguish things that differ.

There are also things you will wish to avoid from your parents' home and relationship. Where there was unhappiness or tension, ask yourself why this was; be on your guard that your own personality does not too closely imitate your parents in those areas.

Question 9 of your assignment is the same as question 8, except that you are now asking: 'What things do I expect my partner to copy from my family home?' For two reasons it must always be wrong to ask question 10. In the first place your partner cannot possibly know what your family home was really like, and therefore to copy it deliberately in any respect is impossible. And secondly, the good things in your family home should be present in your own marriage not because they were true of your parents, but because they are good things for any marriage. In other words, you never expect your husband or wife to be a carbon copy of your parents, they must be allowed to bring themselves as they are to your marriage, governed only by the word of God.

Remember, the girl is not married to her father-in-law, nor the fellow to his mother-in-law. Genesis 2:24 is packed with meaning, which we saw in the last chapter. Whether your own parents' marriage was a dream come true, or a nightmare to forget, you must both work at making yours, your own. Once you are married, take a firm leave of your parents. Be willing to cut off the old traditions and make new ones together. Engagement is a way of telling both families that the leaving and cleaving has begun.

The girl is not married to her father in law, nor the fellow to his mother in law

Making your castle into a home

One of the greatest compliments we have received came from a friend who visited our home and commented: 'I love coming here, it is so relaxing'. We don't always think it is, but we were glad that he did!

What did you conclude at question 11 in your assignment? If you used a dictionary you may not have found it helpful! However, in common usage there is a world of difference between saying 'This is my house' and, 'I feel at home here'. When we invite a friend to 'make yourself at home' we are not offering her the deeds of our house! A house is described in terms of fabric like bricks, timber, glazing and decor; a home refers to the non-material things such as relationships and atmosphere. Although you may not realise it, every home has an atmosphere that can be felt by others.

You can work hard and spend a fortune mixing and matching so that your house becomes a beautiful show-piece, but it may be minus those important ingredients that make it a home. Perhaps you are either fussy or messy, over-organized or disorganized, very quiet or noisy, busy or lazy. You can be sure that we all bring our characteristic traits into our home. If you are always quarrelling, visitors will feel uncomfortable; on the other hand if the wife keeps ordering the husband around, your friends will feel sorry for him and will not want to return.

So whether you live in a house, flat, maisonette, mobile home or whatever, you will need to work hard at making it a welcoming home. But what makes a home? Surely it must be healthy relationships and a warm and welcoming atmosphere. Love and trust that result from obedience to Christ and his word is the Christian plus factor for a good home.

Lowering the drawbridge

There is a love in your relationship that is never to be shared and a love that is to be shared generously. If you turn to your Bible study question 3 you will realise that the family on the fringe is bigger than your immediate relatives. The verses you studied cover those of the household of faith and strangers as well. Hospitality is something that must be part of your life together, or else you are disobedient. The Greek word for hospitality in the New Testament literally means: 'a love of strangers'. So real hospitality is not just entertaining your friends and peer group.

Go through your list again. Don't simply invite your friends in for a meal and assume that is all there is to hospitality. Look around your church, club or community for the people you don't know; and your neighbours. Turn to Luke 14:12-14 and read this passage together. Does this make you re-think your list? What other categories of people should you now add to your hospitality?

Look at your response to the Bible study questions 3 and 4. When it comes to hospitality don't worry about –

Your furniture and your new carpet. Friendship is more important than stain-free fabric. Be relaxed about crumbs and coffee stains.

Your clean home. Never follow visitors around with a dustpan!

Your inexperience. Start simply with coffee and biscuits; the worst cook can manage this.

Your slender finance. Don't commit yourself to big meals. Make sure guests know what they are coming for—'Come for something to eat' meant a finger snack to you, but a three course meal for your guests! Say, 'Come for coffee and cake', if that's what you mean.

Your fear of making conversation with strangers. Just keep asking questions and be interested in what they do.

Add a 'Visitors Book' to your wedding gift list or, if you are already married, buy one for your next anniversary. In years to come you will enjoy looking back over the record of those you have entertained. We have had visitors from every continent and many countries; prayers have been said in different languages during our family devotions, and messages have been written in the book in scripts that we cannot even read! Some of our overseas visitors have cooked their own national meal for us. You receive more than you give when you open your doors and welcome people in. Our lives have been enriched and our knowledge extended as we have entertained many lovely people.

Plan your hospitality and use it to get to know people and help others to grow in their faith. Turn back to question six of your Bible study and remind yourselves of what Aquila and Priscilla did with their home.

What do you do when friends or relatives drop in on Sunday just before you are leaving for church? Or when they come for lunch and seem to take a long time leaving? Our strong advice is that you make it courteously clear right from the start of your marriage that only emergencies are allowed to interfere with your attendance at church. If you ignore the fact that you intended to go to church, it will be impossible to do anything about it when the visits become a habit. Never be afraid of letting relatives and friends know that for you this is important.

It is not a good witness to stay at home during a church service in order to entertain your guests

It really is not too difficult to get round the problem. Make your intentions clear when you give the invitation. Or say to your guests at the lunch table: 'Now can you stay to tea? We have tea about five and leave for church around six; you are more than welcome to join us for the evening service if you would like to'. That makes everything very clear and gives your visitors an easy excuse to remember they have to be home early tonight! You can take exactly the same line when visitors drop in unexpectedly. Don't be embarrassed, don't have whispered conversations in the kitchen, and don't deny your Lord by pretending worship doesn't matter if you have something else on. It is not a good witness to stay at home in order to entertain your guests. Be honest, be courteous, and who knows, they may join you at church! That is the best possible way you could entertain them.

Planning your week

In chapter five we will discuss how best we can plan our budget. Easily as important is the planning of our time. Time wasted is time lost, and time that will have to be accounted for. Your last assignment question pointed to the need to think through the priorities of time in your week. What did you decide? We suggest you pull out a sheet of paper and juggle with those priorities. Start by listing the hours you will spend each week on various items.

There are 168 hours in each week. You have little control over the time you spend at work, including travel time. Then there are, on average, eight hours sleep each night plus eating time. Let's assume all these essential ingredients into your week amount to 113 hours. You can work it out for your situation and produce your own figures; it's a worthwhile exercise. By our reckoning that leaves you with 55 free hours each week! But they are not really free are they? You have already listed some of the things you want to do in that time. Some of it may include a study programme to advance your career.

We ought to place at the top of our list the time we will spend serving God. That is, both in private prayer and Bible reading and in public worship; but it also includes Christian service. However busy your lives are, put God first in your time as in everything. If you are too busy to join with the Christians in prayer and worship and ministry then you are far too busy and you are ignoring the basic pattern of the Christian life that you will find in Acts 2:42.

The remainder of your time you will juggle with household duties, including the car and the garden and following any hobbies you may have. How much do other people figure in your time list? Did you allow any time for hospitality or for just being with your friends?

One thing you must not neglect is your evening together. However busy you are, set aside one evening in the week which you spend together, alone. Whether you stay in or go out doesn't matter; what matters is that you are together. Guard this if you value your marriage. If you keep it regularly now, it will become a natural 'family evening' if children come into your home later.

The purpose of this pencil and paper exercise is not that you should live such regimented lives that you have no time to be real, but that you should identify your priorities of time before circumstances dictate them for you.

Assignment for chapter four

Two into one will go

This assignment should be completed on your own and without reference to your partner. Please do not discuss the questions or your answers until you read the chapter together. Then discuss the assignment only at the point in the chapter when you are recommended to do so.

Whose role?

1 How would you describe your chief responsibility in your future home?

2 What do you consider to be your partner's chief responsibility?

3 Do you find it difficult to make decisions?

4 Who makes most of the decisions in your relationship?

5 Are you happy with this arrangement?

6 Make a list of the regular jobs that will need to be done in your home. Now tick the items that you personally will be responsible for and double-tick jobs to be shared.

Bible Study for chapter four

Two into one will go

It is important that you complete the Bible study before you tackle the chapter. Work through this study separately at first, and without any reference to your partner. Notice that there is one part for the wife and one for the husband.

For the wife
Read Ephesians 5:21-24

1 How do you understand this word 'submit'? Think it through carefully. Can you list some of the practical areas where you expect to show this submission?
2 Make a note of any areas in which you reserve the right not to submit.
3 Do you honestly look forward to the privilege of submitting to your husband?
4 Do you respect him now?

Now read Ephesians 5:25-33

5 List, in order of priority to you, three ways in which you expect your husband to show his love to you.
6 What do verses 26 to 28 mean to you? How do they help to describe the way your partner should treat you?

For the husband
Read Ephesians 5:21-24

7 In what practical ways do you expect your future wife to 'submit' to you?
8 But notice from v.21 that 'submission' works both ways! In what ways will you submit to your wife?
9 The Scripture crowns you as 'head' of the wife. Do you look forward to this responsibility with:
Joy. Anxiety. Bewilderment. Uncertainty. Confidence. Indifference. Pleasure. Apprehension? You may wish to circle more than one.

Now read Ephesians 5:25-33

10 List, in order of priority to you, three ways in which you expect to show your love to your wife.
11 What do verses 26 to 28 mean to you? How do they help you to understand the way you should treat your partner?
Now sit together and, having exchanged papers, carefully go through the questions. If there are surprises in your partner's answers then say so. If you disagree, say so. Discuss why you disagree.

Two into one will go

HAVE YOU WORKED THROUGH THE ASSIGNMENT AND BIBLE STUDY?

In chapter two we were thinking about God's perfect plan for our marriage. It was a high standard, almost frighteningly high. None of us will perfectly match it, but it is good to reach for it. How on earth is it possible for two people, who are two individuals with all their differences of character, interests and habits, to live together and share everything together, as if they were just one? That must be impossible. But marriage is all about two becoming one; and two into one will go.

A marriage is a marvellous thing. A marriage that works is a miracle.

Whose role?

Many marriages fail because one partner or both just does not know what they are supposed to be doing. So let's get the roles clear now. What we have already said in chapter two should begin to show the way. Here is a principle which will point us in the right direction.

★ He is the home-provider.

★ She is the home-maker.

This may not be politically correct today but it is certainly the teaching of the Bible. Here are two verses that clearly prove this. The first is in 1 Timothy 3:4 'One who rules his own house well'. We know that Paul is here referring to Christian leaders, but since the leader is to be an example in all things, the pattern must be true for all. The word 'rule' in vs. 4 and 5 refers not only to his task as head or leader but is used in the sense of protecting, providing and caring. That is the husband's role.

The second verse is found in Titus 2:5 where Paul encourages the young women to be 'homemakers'. The *Authorised Version* of 1611 has 'keepers at home', the *New International Version* has 'busy at home' and back in 1526 William Tyndale quaintly translated it 'huswyfly'—'housewifely'! The word literally means 'the keeper of the house' in the sense of looking after the affairs of the home. We will return to this in more detail later.

Do you see the balance here? He provides and protects so that she can plan and prepare. All the tasks that have to be done in any family can be shared providing the overall pattern of roles is understood. The roles must never be reversed even though tasks may be mixed.

At this point discuss your assignment questions 1 and 2 and see whether your conclusions tie in with what you have just read. The following diagram may help

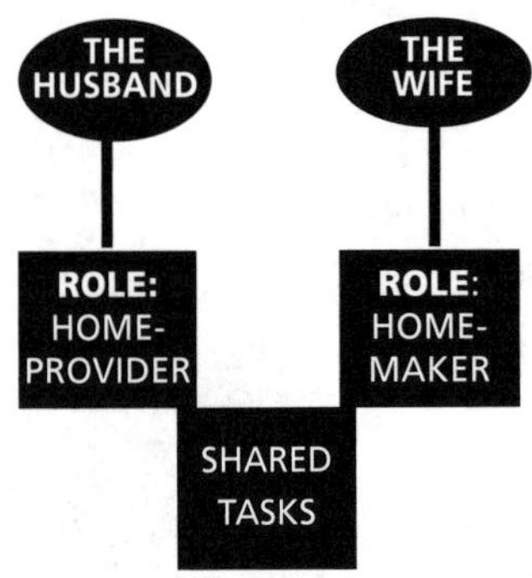

to clarify the distinction between roles and tasks. Remember, this is not the result of centuries of cultural tradition – it is the Bible's view of marriage.

Who does what?

One of the most familiar cries from all walks of life must surely be: 'But I thought you were going to do that!' It happens when there is a lack of communication and no one is too sure who does what. Perhaps you have already discovered this.

Many people are dissatisfied in their work simply because they don't know what they are supposed to be doing. Almost everybody wants some area of their own; something to aim at; something to achieve.

Traditional tasks may be reversed so long as the biblical roles are understood. For example the husband may be a marvellous gourmet or the wife may be brilliant at DIY. More significantly, in today's economic culture it is sometimes possible for the wife to command an income that makes her the chief provider. In some cases she may be the only one who can find employment. If necessity dictates a situation like this, we must never allow the biblical role to be reversed even though the domestic tasks may be mixed. However, the following advice is based upon an understanding of the wife as home-maker and the husband as home-provider.

The wife's responsibilities

Proverbs 31 is often quoted as the ideal picture of the ideal wife. Most people find it hard to accept and even harder to follow. So let's help you out with our own up-date that casts it in a modern style.

v.10. This priceless wife, with an outstanding character, is very difficult to find.
v.11. Her husband has full confidence in her, and in her he has the greatest of riches.
v.12. She brings him good, not harm, throughout his life.
v.13. She chooses quality material and quality items to equip the home and family.
v.14. She shops wisely and plans well in advance for her household.
v.15. She gets up early to prepare the day's food for her family and to ensure that all in her home are provided for.
v.16. She supplements the family income by a careful investment of her resources.
v.17. She works hard and with her whole heart plans every task.
v.18. She is satisfied with all her work, and ensures that her family sleeps securely.
v.19. She looks for ways of being thrifty, making what she need not buy.

v.20. She has a generous heart for the poor, and is always ready to lend a hand to those in need.
v.21. She is not afraid of the cold weather because she has provided enough clothing for her family to keep warm.
v.22. Her own clothes are neat and smart.
v.23. Because of her, her husband is a respected man, and can confidently give good advice to those who seek it.
v.24. She looks for ways of making the budget go further.
v.25. She is strong and trustworthy and because of her diligence can face the future with confidence.
v.26. She speaks wisely and all her words are kind.
v.27. She watches over the affairs of her family and is never idle.
v.28. Her children respect her and her husband praises her.
v.29. He says: 'There are many good and capable wives, but you are an example to them all'.
v.30. Charm is deceptive and beauty passes away; but a woman who fears the Lord is to be praised.
v.31. She will receive the reward she has earned and her good works will speak well of her to everyone.

Some have taken this passage in Proverbs to justify the wife who spends all day away from home pursuing her career, but notice that clearly this woman's home and family hold first priority for her. Everything she does is to provide for her household so that they will be well fed and clothed and secure in her love, wisdom and counsel. Her husband, family, friends and neighbours all speak well of her. What we have here is a reference to a home-maker and home industries, rather than to the career girl. As one commentator has put it: 'Here is scope for formidable powers and great achievements'.

The good home-maker gets up early and prepares breakfast to see the family off to school and work. The home-maker is busy at home. Her purpose is to keep the place healthy and happy. She does not want it to be a palace, where everyone treads with fear, nor a castle, where no-one gets in at all; but a home, where everyone, especially the family, feel welcome.

We have a Sarah Kay poster on the broom cupboard in our kitchen. It is a delightful picture of a quaint housewife sweeping the floor. The caption reads: 'My house is clean enough to be healthy, and dirty enough to be happy'. That is what every home should be. The wife who is a perfectionist or has a fad about cleanliness is misery to live with and turns a home into a sterile hospital theatre. And that is only marginally better than the pig-sty for comfort! Remember that there is a world of difference between house-keeping and home-making. A house consists of bricks, plaster, paint and paper, whereas a home is atmosphere. The home should be so 'homely' that the family looks forward to returning to it each evening.

Part of the task for the home-maker is to plan and prepare the meals. Notice that they have to be planned. To do this, you must plan your shopping. It is a waste of time, effort and money to be shopping every day. Only the bad manager goes out every day for the food for that day. Plan the meals. Don't wait until your husband comes home from work and enquire: 'What do you want for dinner tonight, dear?' The meal should be prepared and you should be ready to welcome him home. This is not to say that a wife will never consult her husband about his preferences, but she will plan ahead.

In the same way, the home-maker should always be at home when the children, and the husband, come home from school and work. Children hate coming home to an empty house. 'Latch-key kids' are the first to get into trouble. The caring, loving, quietly efficient, home-maker, is also an effective peacemaker. Titus 2:4-5 is a lost art among many wives today. Paul encourages Titus to remind the older women to teach the young wives: 'To love their husbands, to love their children, to be discreet, chaste, **homemakers**, good, obedient to their own husbands, that the word of God may not be blasphemed.' It is a tragedy that so many Christians have swallowed the modern secular feminist approach that ridicules such a pattern. It is so important that it is worth quoting the same verse from the NIV: 'The older women can train the younger women to love their husbands and children, to be self-controlled and pure, to **be busy at home**, to be kind, and to be subject to their husbands, so that no one will malign the word of God'.

Another word is used in 1 Timothy 5:14 to describe the wife's duties. It is translated '**manage the house**', and in the NIV 'manage their homes'. The word is made up from two words: 'house' and 'master'. You may be interested to know that in classical Greek this word was used to describe the influence of the planets controlling human lives. That represented some influence! In Mark 14:14, the word refers to the 'master of the house'. Here in 1 Timothy 5:14 it refers to the wife. This is all much more than the modern idea of 'housework'.

To be a good home-maker there must be planning and preparation. If you are hopeless at planning, hate cooking and housework, and dread the thought of leaving work and running a home, then you have two options to choose from:

Get help quick, or cancel your wedding date!

In her book *The Role of Women* (IVP 1984) Elizabeth Catherwood remarks that as a result of feminist publicity, 'no word is more laden with the aura of boredom, lack of ability and character, or even sheer horror, than that of "housewife".' Sadly Elizabeth Catherwood is right.

Some years ago, the head of a girl's High School was being interviewed on the radio. She lamented girls having no drive for top management: 'There is no doubt at all', she complained, 'babies and the home knock the fight out of a girl'. What a miserably one-sided and inadequate view of the home-maker. The wife, mother and home-maker is already in top management!

One day a mother was out shopping with a baby in the pram and two toddlers dragging behind. A young woman approached from the opposite direction. Smartly dressed, she had obviously reached the top of her profession. As she drew near, the mother recognised her as an old school friend. 'Hello', the professional greeted, 'and what are you doing in life?' The weary mother pulled herself upright and responded: 'I'm working in a partnership for social development and I supervise the 'under-five's' department. I also spend a fair bit of my time in the department of health, hygiene and food, and assist in financial control. What do you do?' 'Oh', gasped the admiring young professional, 'I'm just a model'. That is how every wife and mother should view her position—top management.

Every wife and mother should view her role as top management

We have heard people say: 'I wouldn't know what to do all day at home; I would be bored.' If you think like this you have forgotten what an exciting, challenging and fulfilling role a home-maker has. But more important than this, it is God's role for the wife: to be obedient to his plan provides the best excitement, challenge and fulfilment.

If the thought of being involved with the home and family frightens you, or bores you, read Proverbs 31 again and see the many aspects of life you could include when you are your own boss in home-making. Look especially at verse 20, and discuss how this can extend to working within the local church. Any healthy church could use an army of home-makers who care for others.

The husband's responsibilities

It may similarly appear old-fashioned to say that the husband is the chief bread-winner, but as we have already seen from 1 Timothy 3:4 that is God's pattern. It is also implied in God's punishment at the Fall: 'Cursed is the ground for your sake; in toil you shall eat from it all the days of your life... In the sweat of your face you shall eat bread.' (Genesis 3:17-19). Again, this is the biblical pattern and problems can easily arise when the pattern is broken; therefore extra care is needed when, for reasons of health or unemployment the chief tasks have to be reversed.

Generally, it is the husband who finds himself as Mr Fixit. And if you can't, then you should start buying some good books that will help you, or taking some lessons. Find a good and experienced friend to advise you. Never be too proud to ask advice, other men just love sharing their expertise! Better than anything is to join some of the church working-parties; you will learn a vast amount under the direction of some of the real handymen in the church.

In the realm of finance, which we shall look at in more detail in the next chapter, the wife may be better at book-keeping, but the husband must lead in strategy and decision making. It is part of his responsibility never to let his wife worry over money matters. As the home-provider, the husband is also Lord Protector! His job is to save his wife from worrying; just as her job is to save him from worry! But keeping a wife from worry does not mean keeping her in the dark; that only increases her anxiety. What it does mean is steering the home away from problems and helping to manage the big decisions in a wise and responsible way. If the wife is the book-keeper make sure you regularly discuss the state of the finances with her. Few wives want a husband who never knows how much there is in the bank.

Leadership and decision making are inseparable. Discuss together your responses to the assignment questions 4,5,6. Who comes out on top as far as making decisions is concerned in your relationship? In every marriage there are continually decisions to be made, ranging from what company you will buy your electricity from, to whether it is time to change the car. Most decisions will be mutually agreed after discussion, but there is an ultimate responsibility—and it lies with the husband. It is an abdication of his role if he is constantly saying, 'You decide, dear'. Even worse when he allows his wife to make the decisions and then, when something goes wrong, he accuses, 'Well it wasn't my idea in the first place.' A husband is equally wrong when he never consults his wife on anything.

We saw from our leadership diagram in chapter two that the husband should be the spiritual leader, caring for his wife's spiritual life, guarding his own, and making sure that they both grow together in Christ. Ecclesiastes 4:9,10: 'Two are better than one...If one falls down, his friend can help him up' (NIV). In chapter two also, we thought about the husband as the wife's pastor. Don't overlook this, it is a significant part of your responsibility.

During the early years of marriage it is often necessary for both partners to go out to work. Naturally this throws some of the duties into disorder. Nevertheless, aim at the ideal and don't allow the 'wife-at-work' pattern to go on for too long; if it does, you will discover that it becomes a perpetual necessity to your family income. Right from the start we advise that you plan for the wife to leave work.

When you are both at work, remember that duties (tasks) should be shared. But don't forget the responsibilities. The wife is still in charge of homemaking.

Plan together, work together, talk together. No young wife should come home after a full day's work, prepare the evening meal and get on with the housework and washing, whilst her husband lounges in the armchair with the newspaper, convincing himself that he has earned an evening off.

If the wife must work, the husband must pay for it!

Who does the garden?

Compare the lists you both drew up for question 6 of your assignment. It doesn't matter that these are not complete lists; you wouldn't expect them to be at this stage. The point is, have you noticed any items where you each considered that you were responsible? This just underlines the importance of discussion and negotiation.

It is no good dreaming about a lovely garden. Even since Adam and Eve spoilt everything, a good garden demands hard work. You would be wise to decide how you will tackle this problem. Perhaps you will discover that it was a flat you wanted after all! We are not talking about rigid boundaries of jobs, or that you each have to drop into the traditional pattern expected of you. But, as we said earlier; each of you will want some areas of responsibility that are your own. And when these have been worked out there is no need to consult your partner on every detail. Get on with your job.

Giving up your Independence

One of the most shattering experiences of marriage is to discover what it means to lose your independence. Never again can you think of yourself in isolation; you cannot plan where you holiday, what you buy, or even what you eat, without having your partner in mind. The longer you have been single, the harder this loss of independence becomes.

However, lose it you must, because you are no longer two but one. Your vocabulary must change from the first person singular 'I', to the first person plural 'we'. Similarly your thinking must change from 'me', to 'us'. The traditions and patterns of your life must be abandoned or at least re-shaped. You cannot expect your partner to adopt all your peculiarities any more than you need to embrace theirs. Too many marriages fall at this hurdle because one partner or both insists on living just as they used to when no one else shared their heart, home and bed.

You cannot expect your partner to adopt all your peculiarities any more than you need to embrace theirs.

If you are not prepared to lose your independence, you dare not marry, because marriage is a partnership that must not be dissolved until death. In future your best interests are to please your partner and that will be your priority for perhaps fifty years or more.

In your Bible Study for this chapter you may have spent some time with the idea of 'submission'. Tricky isn't it? But it must be part of this idea of losing independence. We dealt with the principle of this in chapter two – now for the practice. Submission for the wife is a recognition of and respect for his leadership in the partnership. But recognition is more than just acknowledging the biblical teaching; it is a practical willingness to be led by him. But how does this work out? Here are a few pointers:

First, the wife must support her husband's spiritual leadership in the home.

Secondly, when you reach an impasse in a decision that has to be made the husband must make the decision and can expect his wife's support.

Thirdly, a submissive wife will always speak respectfully about and to her husband and will never criticise him behind his back or in company.

Fourthly, submission also implies organising the home to provide the best support for the demands of his daily work.

Of course there are exceptions to this whole area of submission. If a husband expects his wife to act contrary to the teaching of the Bible or if he makes unreasonable demands by treating his wife cruelly, she is not bound to obey. Submission does not imply slavery. But remember Paul commands 'submit to one another'. That means the husband also has a submissive role! Again, a few points:

First, the husband should make his plans in the light of his wife's needs and preferences; recall what we said about 'living considerately' in chapter two.

Secondly, he will always speak to her and about her with warmth and courtesy.

Thirdly, he will listen to her counsel and comments with respect for feminine wisdom and intuition.

Fourthly, he will never stubbornly insist on his own way to the hurt of his wife; he will gladly be inconvenienced for her convenience.

Perhaps all this has given you both a new approach to this subject of submission. Rather than something to be grudgingly given or dictatorially demanded it provides a perfect balance for the perfect marriage. It is to be enjoyed not feared. It is a Christian mind-set not a destructive minefield.

Remaining an individual

At first sight, the idea of remaining an individual may seem to be a contradiction of what we have just said, but one writer on this subject refers to 'Space in your togetherness'. Think about that because it is very important. However much you are one, you are still two individuals. Two bodies, two minds, two personalities, two souls. In brief, you are two bundles of separateness. That is far too important to overlook.

Trust your partner to be an individual. Treat your partner with respect and allow some privacy. Never open each other's mail. You may share ninety-nine percent of it immediately, but don't spoil the fun by opening the catalogue that describes the present he is buying you for your birthday, or the letter confirming that surprise weekend away he has planned for you both. More seriously, there may be unkind and hurtful, or confidential, letters that one partner needs to share with the other at the right time and in the right way.

Some couples insist that they trust each other and have therefore agreed to open each other's mail; but if you think about it for a minute, there is more trust in **not** opening each others mail. Never enquire: 'Who is writing to you from Wiltshire then?' The thought-response is always: 'She doesn't trust me'. On the other hand don't be unnecessarily secretive about your mail. Share what you can at once and that should be almost all of it.

Never rummage through your partner's handbag or wallet, purse or drawer. Each of you should have a drawer or shelf for personal items. It's not that that area is forbidden territory, simply that you choose to respect a little privacy in each other's life. That is trust. The big things are all shared, but let your partner have some little privacies—a little space in your togetherness. Don't suffocate each other.

Let your partner have a little space in your togetherness

A wife should rarely have cause to telephone her husband at work and she must never get in the habit of phoning him with every problem. It can surely wait until he comes home in the evening. But don't phone your mother as a substitute either!

There are some good reasons why a husband should never get in the habit of 'phoning his wife from work each day:

★ Because there is no need to.
★ Because it is a dishonest habit. Your firm is paying for the call.
★ Because you are checking up. You appear not to be trusting her.
★ Because you will worry when she is out when you expected her to be in, and when you get home you will be quizzing her about it.
★ Because she thinks you think she is not capable of managing a day without your advice.

Jealousy can kill a marriage. Be careful that it does not kill yours. On your wedding day you make some serious vows, promising to keep yourselves only for each other; so trust each other with these promises and when one of you wants to make a call on a friend, or attend an evening class, gladly let them do it. Be on your guard that you do not resent every conversation your partner has with someone of the opposite sex. Don't 'smother' your partner, give them some space; you need to be able to breathe freely from each other from time to time and you don't have to do everything together.

Assignment for chapter five

Money matters

This assignment should be completed on your own and without reference to your partner. Please do not discuss the questions or your answers until you read the chapter together. Then discuss the assignment only at the point in the chapter when you are recommended to do so.

Money matters

1 List your personal hobbies/interests.

2 List the hobbies/interests of your partner.

3 How much time and money do you each spend on your personal hobby/interest each week?

4 Do you often go shopping together?

5 At this particular moment do you know approximately/accurately how much you have in the bank or building society?

6 Do you know approximately/accurately what your partner has in the bank or building society?

7 How do you rate your attitude to money?
Careless. Extravagant. Generous. Mean. Cautious. Careful.

8 How do you rate your partner's attitude to money?
Careless. Extravagant. Generous. Mean. Cautious. Careful.

9 Have you discussed your future finances in detail?

10 Where will you find the money to buy a birthday present for your husband/wife when you are married?

Bible Study for chapter five

Money matters

It is important that you complete the Bible study before you tackle the chapter.
Find some unhurried time and work it through together.

Part 1

2 Corinthians 8 and 9 are key chapters on the way Christians should give their money to help others. Read through these two chapters. Now return and in each of the following verses think of one word only that describes the manner of the Corinthians' giving. In some verses you could think of more than one word but in your **complete** list avoid using a word more than once. We have suggested the first two for you. When you read the chapter you can check your results against ours – but come up with your own suggestions first!

2 Corinthians 8

v.2 joyfully
v.3 sacrificially
v.7
v.8
v.12
v.14
v.19
v.21

2 Corinthians 9

v.2
v.5
v.7
v.11

Part 2

Look up the following verses and in a simple sentence for each passage explain what it means to you. We suggest that you work from the *New International Version* here.

Proverbs 23:4-5
Proverbs 11:24-25
Haggai 1:6
Malachi 3:8

Money matters

More than half of all the parables told by our Lord contain stories about money or wealth. Is this because both are an important part of our life? Perhaps we have little and long for more, or we may have a lot and are frightened of losing it. Either way what is certain is that we all need some.

HAVE YOU WORKED THROUGH THE ASSIGNMENT AND BIBLE STUDY?

Excessive wealth or poverty are the causes of tension in many marriages. In three quarters of all marriage failures finance is identified as a significant cause. Paul's warning in 1Timothy 6:10 'the love of money is a root of all kinds of evil' is a well-known saying even among those who are unaware that it comes from the Bible. But as Christians we ought to be aware of the context, which in fact begins in verse 6.

Because of the importance of this subject we have devoted a whole chapter to it.

Discuss together your assignment answers. Talk through the questions and see how in touch with your finances you both are. Stop over on that question 10 for a while. Have you thought of this before? Have you got an answer to it? If you have got an answer, can you think of any snags in your idea? We will return to this before we close this chapter. You will need to be very honest with each other on questions 7 and 8! But if you have any doubts about this area, now is the time to talk.

When you are choosing your house and what to put in it, keep in mind Proverbs 15:27, 'A greedy man brings trouble to his family' (NIV). A home is more important than its contents. You don't have to walk into a prepared palace. It's fun building a home together.

Once you are married you will no longer need separate bank and building society accounts for general expenses. One joint account with either signature will work well enough. Some young couples start this even before they are married, but it is certainly not advisable to start before you are engaged, and even then it can be complicated and very distressing if the engagement breaks off. If you are going to start a joint-account before you get married then seek some professional advice from a solicitor, bank manager or some other wise financial adviser.

Some time before your wedding day, and certainly before you start negotiating to buy or rent a house, you need to sit down and work out your expenditure in great detail. This must be a full 'board meeting' of both of you. You will need a whole, unhurried evening with plenty of paper and coffee to hand. It will be best if you have done a little homework before you sit down.

At this meeting of the exchequer, dreams get converted into pounds and pence—or Euros!

As you read this, you may have been married for a few months or even years. Perhaps you have your finances well under control; on the other hand you may already be afraid that you are not making ends meet and the debts are mounting. Either way we believe this next section will help you considerably.

We have ranged the following list in order of priority as we see it, and it should cover every major expenditure. Work through it in order and don't dodge about.

The Lord's treasury

In every part of the life of the Christian that which belongs to God comes first. For this reason we begin our list with the amount of our income that will be given to the work of the gospel. Our Bible study focused on the way we give to God's work. The Corinthians were giving to relieve the poverty of their fellow Christians in Judea. Our giving will be wider than simply famine relief. At this point check through the results of your Bible study on 2 Corinthians 8 and 9. Here is our list for comparison, but it is not exhaustive. If you dig deeper into these chapters you will find much more on the subject of giving.

2 Corinthians 8

v.2 joyfully
v.3 sacrificially
v.7 abundantly
v.8 sincerely or lovingly
v.12 willingly or freely
v.14 equally
v.19 readily or eagerly
v.21 honourably

2 Corinthians 9

v.2 zealously or enthusiastically
v.5 bountifully or generously
v.7 cheerfully
v.11 liberally

Many Christians tithe their income. This means they give one tenth to God. Although there is no law about this for the Christian, there is good Old Testament precedent for it—see for example Leviticus 27:30-33. Some of us reason that we do not want to give less under the gospel of grace than the Jews gave under the Old Testament law. But whatever you decide on this matter, you must fix a percentage and keep to it. You may like to take 1 Corinthians 16:1-2 as a guide also. You must talk over whether your proportion is to be taken from your gross or net income.

Don't move on through the list until this one is sorted out. Put God's portion right at the top. Give to him first. Never allow yourselves to say: 'We can't afford to give to God's work yet, we have so many expenses; we will start in a few years time'. If you talk like this, we can guarantee that you will never be able to afford to give to God. Look back on your explanation of Malachi 3:8. Remember that God will honour those who honour him.

Plan your giving in terms of a percentage, not just a sum of money. Then each year you can review, and consider the possibility of a percentage point rise.

Mortgage or rent

This will be a major outgoing and you will be ready to fit a figure in here as soon as you are thinking of your first home. As an interim measure you can always ask for an estimate from a trusted advisor in finance, or some friends who have just entered the market.

Council Tax

You may be paying this already, but if you are moving to another area, you will be advised to check out what the rate is likely to be under the new authority. Don't forget to claim a rebate if you have paid in advance and then move from your local authority.

Water and Sewerage charges. You can't avoid them.

Gas/electricity

You will need to take some advice on this. Don't just make a wild guess because you may be wildly wrong. Ask a couple in similar circumstances.

Insurance

It is unwise to go through life uninsured just because you think you cannot afford it. However tight your budget, afford some insurance at least. If you are buying a house through a bank or building society you will have no option but to insure the buildings, but the contents are your own responsibility. How could you afford to replace your contents after fire, theft or accidental damage? Work out the value of the contents of your home at replacement cost and you will be surprised just how much you are worth! What about life insurance? Your mortgage will be covered, but how will a wife and young family manage if the husband dies unexpectedly? Or, for that matter, how will the husband provide care for young children if the wife dies? Remember, insurance is never as cheap as now.

Food and household items

Work this out together and try to be as accurate as you can. Again you may find some friends to help here; but be careful to know what they include in the food bill. After all, you may have friends who dine out three times a week, or eat fresh salmon every Sunday. Don't forget to include household cleaning items. The figure you arrive at for food and household items may need to be adjusted after a few months trial, but once agreed stick to it as your budget. Don't just go to the supermarket and buy food. Keep within your allowance.

Telephone and, if you must have one, television

We recommend that at least for the first two years of your life together you do not have a television. Without it you will be forced to talk together, and who knows, you may find it such fun that you will never want one. Watch those telephone bills. Whatever the adverts say, talking is expensive!

Car costs

A car is a major item in the family expenditure. It is vital therefore that you adequately budget for it. Tax, insurance, servicing, and depreciation are all additional to your fuel costs. If you receive a work-related mileage allowance, remember that it is intended to assist the running and replacement of your car.

Clothes, cosmetics and toiletries

Plan a clothing budget for each of you.

Presents

We do not mean presents for each other, which we will come to later, but for relatives and friends. You would be advised to decide who you will buy presents for and how much you will spend; then divide this for a monthly budget.

Hobbies and holidays

It is unreasonable for one partner, usually the husband, to indulge in an expensive hobby that consumes time and money from the family budget. The fairest agreement is that each partner can use an equal amount of time and money in a hobby or interest of their choice. Ideally you will share the same interest, but this is not essential providing equality is agreed from the start. Holidays can be expensive. Don't wait until you are about to fly out to Tasmania before wondering where the money will come from. Never borrow to pay for a holiday.

House maintenance

You will need to budget for repairs and redecoration both of which are very expensive. Remember that whether you are renting or buying a leasehold property, there will almost certainly be contractual obligations placed on you to redecorate periodically.

Garden care

On a very tight budget this must be your lowest priority for expense, however much you dream of a neat and colourful garden. A few well-selected ground cover plants can stifle weeds and save hours of work. Growing your own vegetables may sound very exciting and 'green', but it is never economical either in time or money. Of course, the garden may be the hobby of either or both of you in which case you will have more to spend.

Contingency

There is always something unexpected that comes up. Save regularly for this.

Personal allowances

Although this is almost at the bottom of our list, it is absolutely vital. What was your conclusion at question 10 on your assignment? We strongly recommend that you set aside an agreed and equal weekly or monthly personal allowance for each of you. This will cover such things as your individual hobbies, your presents for each other, and any other bits and pieces you may want to buy. It is possibly the best way of ensuring that neither partner overspends the family budget on expensive hobbies or personal luxuries. There are few things more discouraging to the young husband who, after much careful thought, has bought his wife the first birthday present of their marriage than to be met with: 'What on earth did you buy that for? You know we can't afford that much.' If it comes from his own personal allowance then it is no business of hers how much it cost.

This allowance is even more essential when the wife stops her paid employment. She should never be made to feel that she must ask for some pocket money from her husband. Still worse is to hear of the wife who is saving for a special present for her husband by economising week by week from the food bill. Incidentally, a husband who threatens or even jokes that he will stop the housekeeping as some kind of punishment, is insulting his wife and family. The housekeeping allowance is not charity that she receives from the generosity of her husband, it is essential for his own well-being as well as hers. If the wife buys the food, she is merely the executive for that aspect of the common purse. She is, remember, the manager of the home.

This personal allowance must be received regularly by each partner. To accommodate this you can open your own bank or building society account, or use it in any way you wish. This is a private account if you want it to be so. It is a little more space in your togetherness.

Savings

The Christian organization Credit Action tells us that Mr Average has only enough savings to keep him going for three weeks. At first your budget may be so tight that there is very little, if any, left over for saving. However, it is part of Christian stewardship to make provision for the unexpected wherever this is possible; look up 1 Timothy 5:8 where the words 'provide for' mean 'to plan beforehand'. In Matthew 6:25-34, and v.34 in particular, our Lord warns about unnecessary and unproductive anxiety; he is not making a case against wise preparation for the future.

When you are able to save, it is well to remember that it will pay you to save in an account in the wife's name as soon as she leaves work. She will not be paying income tax and the interest gained will therefore be higher.

Having sorted all this out, be ready to re-negotiate the whole package within the first six months of marriage. That allows for two quarters' bills. Reality will change the picture considerably. Discuss together all major departures from this plan. If each keeps to the rules there should never be any cause for the accusation: 'It's all your fault, look at the mess you've got us into'.

In spite of the pressures from society, children need a full-time mother

Plan for the wife to stop work

Unless otherwise agreed by you both, the wife should never just go on and on working. To avoid this you must plan for the time when you will no longer have her income. Read Proverbs 23:4: 'Do not wear yourself out to get rich; have the wisdom to show restraint' (NIV).

Why is it so important that the wife does not go on working for ever? Because it is hard to have a real home while the wife is out at work all day.

Besides this, the arrival of a baby may upset your best laid plans, so take into account the possibility of starting a family within two or three years. After all, this is hopefully part of your expectation from marriage. In spite of the pressures from society, children need a full-time mother. A day-nursery can never take the place of a loving, caring mother. Cut back on holidays, luxuries or anything else, but don't deprive your children of a full-time mother if at all possible.

You will also get too used to that second income and eventually you will convince yourselves that you cannot manage without it. Read together Ecclesiastes 5:10: 'Whoever loves money never has money enough; whoever loves wealth is never satisfied with his income' (NIV).

Keep in touch with your accounts

There is a biblical proverb that is most relevant when it comes to managing our finance. Proverbs 27:23: 'Be diligent to know the state of your flocks, and attend to your herds'. That is not merely a piece of sound advice to the agricultural community, it simply means keep in touch with the state of your accounts!

To do this, of course, you will need to keep careful records. If you are not doing so already, or neither of you is familiar with how to set about some simple book-keeping, then we strongly advise you to seek help from a Christian accountant, bank manager or other financial adviser. You should be able at all times to see how much you have in the bank or the building society. If you go into the red beyond what is already agreed then hold everything and re-plan immediately. Did you pass the test at the assignment questions 5 and 6? If you would have to ask the bank how much money you have, then you are not in charge of your finances.

Plastic money

Probably more Christians get into financial trouble through the misuse of credit cards than in any other way. So this next section is vital, and to act on it now may save you a great deal of heartache later. Use your credit card with great care. How should you use it? Here are three rules to guarantee you never allow the temptations of plastic money to get you into trouble:

First. Every time you use your credit card make a note in your account book and reckon that money as already spent.

Secondly. Never use your card to pay debts you cannot comfortably cover from your income within the next four weeks. Don't look at your card as an easy way to borrow extra money; it is, but it is one of the most expensive ways also.

Thirdly. If you cannot handle your credit card in line with the two points above, cut it in half and cancel any future cards.

Unless you require them for business purposes, you will normally only need one card account. The more different cards you hold, the more the temptation grows. It is nothing more than social snobbery to flash around a whole wallet of cards.

You would be wise to find a trusted Christian adviser for your financial commitments. Unfortunately you will soon be bombarded with companies assuring you that you are such a valued person that they would love the privilege of lending you some money. Throw all such literature straight in the bin and stick to your adviser. Certainly ignore the sharks that cruise around the high street looking for young people to lend money to. We have known Christians who were persuaded to borrow money they didn't need and then they deposited it in the bank to earn interest far below the rate they were paying on the borrowed money! Unbelievable, but it happens.

Remember it is a fundamental law of finance that the day of reckoning will come—and that's not only a law of finance either!

If you do find yourselves running into financial problems, don't panic, but don't ignore the problem either. Problems never just disappear, they merely grow in complexity. All your difficulties can be solved if you take wise advice, and take it early.

Making a will

Making a will may be the furthest thing from your mind at a time like this! All your plans are for many happy years together. But a will is inexpensive, easy and essential. It is essential at this time for a number of reasons:

First, if one of you should die unexpectedly, a will makes sorting out the financial affairs so much easier for the surviving partner.

Secondly, if you both died together—and it does happen—where would your money and your property go? (Officially called your 'estate') In a will you can decide who gets it and you can leave a proportion to Christian causes of your choice. A will in this instance can save a lot of family squabbling.

Thirdly, if you left a young family orphaned, who would look after them? Your clear instructions can be left in a will. But do discuss your plans first with everyone concerned and take professional advice. Some young couples have a mutual arrangement with another couple in similar circumstances.

Finally

There is a law at work in all pay-packets that goes like this: 'Expenditure increases to accommodate the income', which means, the more you have, the more you spend. As Christians we ought to decide what is a reasonable standard of living and then ask the Lord what he would like us to do with the rest! You will have discovered from Haggai 1:6 that money is soon gone and it does not satisfy, and from Proverbs 23:4-5 that riches are unstable and uncertain. It was left to Malachi 3:8 to remind us of our responsibility towards God in handling our finances.

As you begin your married life you can never be certain how things will turn out for you financially. You may be well-off or struggling. Either way never argue over money and keep God at the centre of your possessions.

Perhaps now is the time to make Proverbs 30:8-9 your prayer, 'Keep falsehood and lies far from me; give me neither poverty nor riches, but give me only my daily bread. Otherwise, I may have too much and disown you and say, "Who is the Lord?" Or I may become poor and steal, and so dishonour the name of my God' (NIV).

Assignment for chapter six

Dealing with differences and coping with crises

This assignment should be completed on your own, without reference to your partner and before you read the chapter. Please do not discuss the questions or your answers together until you reach that point in the chapter when you are recommended to do so.

1 What is there about your partner that you would like to see changed when you are married?

2 What do you think must change in your own life to help make your marriage work?

3 Would you still marry your partner if you knew now that nothing would change in his or her character and habits over the next twenty years?

4 List three things that annoy you most about your partner.

5 List three things about yourself that you think annoy your partner.

6 Tick which of these is true about your partner:

When we disagree my partner's response is :

To turn the issue into a row

To nag until I give in

To listen carefully to my position before answering

To go moody and silent

To ignore my views entirely

To give in and follow me

To refuse to discuss at all

Bible Study for chapter six

Dealing with differences and coping with crises

You should work on this Bible study together. Try to find some unhurried time. ***It is important that you complete the Bible study before you read the chapter.***

Read James 4:1-3. Work through these verses together.
Tragically, these verses describe many marriages today, including some between professing Christians.
1 Short of physical blows, can you list three ways in which a husband and wife can 'fight' each other?
2 What are some of the 'desires for pleasure' that can cause tension in a marriage?
3 One word sums up the first half of verse 2, 'selfishness'. Can you list three practical examples of selfishness that could spoil your marriage?
4 Do you think we can ever be walking closely with God if our marriage is not right?

Now for a positive picture! Read together Galatians 5:22-23.
For each word Paul uses to present the fruit of the Spirit, write a **short** sentence to describe how you hope this would be worked out in practice in your marriage. We suggest you take it in turns to make the first suggestion; this way neither of you will dominate the conclusions. Make sure that every answer is a positively good thing that you describe.
Love:
Joy:
Peace:
Long-suffering:
Kindness:
Goodness:
Faithfulness:
Gentleness:
Self-control:

Dealing with differences and coping with crises

Marriage is the miracle of making opposites compatible and differences similar. Let's draw an imaginary picture of Jack and Jill: They are deeply in love; it is that romantic love that we talked about in chapter one. The sparklers and fizz kind of love. They are high on each other. Jack and Jill are convinced that everything will be OK in their marriage. They have never talked in depth about marriage because they are so sure that all will be well. Their love will conquer all. At first it does, but within a few months, or even a few weeks of their new life together the differences begin to show up.

They thought that because they were both Christians, their religious standards would be the same. They thought that because they came from decent homes, their social habits would be the same. They thought that because they got on so well, their health habits would be similar also. They thought everything would just fit in. That was the problem with Jack and Jill, they thought, but they didn't talk .

Jill discovered that Jack had a habit of relaxing in front of the television all Sunday afternoon; this she found deeply offensive. Jill saw nothing wrong with an occasional glass of wine, but Jack had been brought up in a strict tee-total household.

Jack soon learned that Jill was mad on cats. He always knew that she liked them, but he objected strongly when she brought home two beautiful kittens and insisted that they should sleep on the end of the bed at night.

Jack suffered from smelly feet, and no way could he be encouraged to change his socks daily. He also came in and threw his coat on the stairs. Jill had a fad about tidiness.

Jill had the infuriating habit of boiling the vegetables without the lids on. Jack was very economy minded and knew that this was a waste of gas. Then Jack preferred his fried bread crisp, whilst Jill enjoyed hers soaked in the fat; it was hard to do both in the pan at the same time, and such a waste of time to fry the bread separately!

Jack always assumed that Jill would keep the garden in trim. He hated gardening, and his father never did it. Then Jack discovered that Jill hated the job also. Even worse, Jack's mother was an excellent old fashioned cook and he was used to real English home-cooking. Unfortunately for him, Jill had no interest in mother's cuisine and would settle for a take-away or frozen pie every time. They compromised by eating out a few evenings each week—until they discovered the budget wasn't stretching that far.

In home decorating, Jack was all for anaglypta on the walls, covered with a splash of emulsion; it made redecorating so easy. Jill loved big flower patterns, and never bothered about the amount of work involved.

Jill went into the bathroom each morning and fumed because the towels were all over the floor, and the toothpaste had been squeezed from the middle and the cap left off. Jack, on the other hand, complained that it was a ridiculous habit unrolling the toilet paper from the bottom of the roll, because his mother always set it up to be unrolled from the top.

It seemed that every day when Jack came home from work his mother-in-law had arrived. She had 'just popped in to see Jill'. She had always 'just popped in', and she was always 'just going'. But somehow she nearly always got invited for tea and stayed the evening.

Jack could never make decisions and had to be prodded and nagged if he was to do anything around the house, or make any forward plans.

At a far deeper level, they discovered problems in the bedroom. Jill had never wanted babies; she had a great fear of the responsibility and the pain involved, and was terrified at the thought of conceiving. Jack wanted a large family; he had set his mind on at least ten children!

It was all right for a while. Their love could conquer all, but then...

Turn to your assignment and exchange papers. Spend a few minutes reading carefully and thoughtfully your partner's answers and then discuss any points of difference. Be very honest together, but don't argue! The point about question 1 is that you cannot guarantee anything will change in your partner's character or habits; you marry the person they are now, not the person they may become. Right now you may reassure each other that your love is so strong that you will gladly accept the things you dislike. But when you go home and you are on your own think about it carefully. The issues may be fairly trivial or they may be significant. If they worry you a lot, don't ignore the problem—talk.

If your partner draws your attention to a habit or trait that annoys them, remember that your greatest happiness will be found in their greatest happiness—so do something about it! Think about your future in this way: Nothing may change in my partner's life, but everything must change in mine. If you **both** work on that basis then you are laying a strong foundation.

Turn to your Bible Study assignment and remind yourselves of this great fact: *Selfishness kills a marriage.*

Different differences

'I want' is the attitude that hurts marriage more than anything else. One of the most important responses in dealing with differences and disagreements is to learn how to rate their importance. We can spend days arguing over irrelevancies, blowing them up out of all proportion and using them as a cover-up for the big issues which are left unspoken. But the big ones are the ones that are slowly destroying our relationship. We want to show you what we mean by learning to rate the importance of things that cause disagreements.

Trivialities (or, toilet rolls and toothpaste)

Marriages are full of trivialities, and sadly, full of arguments over those trivialities—things that don't really matter. What happens is that during the months or years of engagement we are on our 'best behaviour' most of the time. Besides, we convince ourselves that we will gladly overlook the annoying habits that, at the present, we do know about. Unfortunately there are many more than we thought, and some of them can only be learnt when you are actually living with someone.

Marriage will do something that engagement will never do. It will show you the very worst about your partner. Maybe they adore pets that you hate. Check out that one now. Never say about anything: 'Oh, we'll talk about that when we are married'. That is much too late. If you can't agree now, what makes you think you will agree then?

There may be food fads that you can afford to overlook during engagement since neither of you is doing all the cooking, but they can be very annoying when a young wife has to please a fussy husband. If you have fads as distinct from allergies, work at changing for your partner's sake. Don't deprive your partner of their favourite food just because you could not be bothered to take the bones out of fish when you were a child!

Then there are habits that are very unpleasant to live with: noisy eating habits, coughing, sniffing, door slamming, nail biting, nervous giggling. The list is endless. There are phobias: anything from spiders to thunderstorms. Some habits you can never discover until you are married: like the night-time disruptions of snoring, talking in your sleep, sleep-walking, thrashing around, and that most desperate cause of disagreement—grabbing the duvet for yourself!

Whenever your partner annoys you and you are secretly fuming, talk. This is the purpose of your assignments for each chapter, to make sure you are talking together. When there is an issue of disagreement, ask each other, and above all ask yourself: 'Does it really matter?' If the honest answer is 'No', then you be the one to give in.

Use your common sense. Sometimes the issue may be one of straightforward economy. No young marriage can afford to be wasteful, so talk about the economics, and the wasteful partner must come in line. Help your partner humorously. Sometimes a little note left in the right place can change a bad habit without causing a hurt. We once had a family problem in the bathroom. It was all about toothpaste and toothbrushes; the following note stuck beside the mirror went a long way to solving a trivial problem:

When you clean your teeth each day,
To improve your looks,
Squeeze the tube the proper way
And keep in dad's good books.

Instructions here for ever stand,
(Andrew, Steve, and Mummy),
When you take the tube in hand
Squeeze toes and not its tummy!

Another point I should have said
When scrubbing teeth you're at.
This tube has tummy, toes and head,
So please replace its hat.

If your partner leaves papers and magazines all over the place, you can approach the problem in one of two ways. You can try screaming: 'Do you think this house is a pig-sty or something? I spend all day cleaning up, and five minutes after you get in anyone would think a bomb had hit us'. Or you could try: 'Darling, it does get at me to see papers and periodicals everywhere; do you think it would be a good idea if we bought a paper-rack?' Don't just go and buy one, get an agreement first.

'I know, I'm sorry, I forgot', goes a long way to heal a tricky situation

When you know you are in the wrong, and your partner has made a reasonable case against you, don't be afraid to admit it. 'I know, I'm sorry, I forgot', goes a long way to heal a tricky situation—and takes the steam out of anyone's boiler! Work hard at the things that annoy your partner. All we have learnt from the Bible comes into play here. 'Submission' and 'living with understanding', are just as relevant in the trivial issues. It is often the trivialities that many couples spend hours squabbling about, and a little thing can wreck a marriage. The second part of your Bible study assignment will have provided sufficient reasons why trivialities should never threaten your marriage.

Keep to the point when you are discussing these comparatively minor matters. If you are arguing over which end to squeeze the toothpaste, never bring in more serious issues, 'and that reminds me, will you stop inviting your mother for tea every Sunday'!

Turmoil (or, cars and cookers)

These are the more important issues that can bring strong disagreement. Once again, you must realise that they are important, and once again, you must keep talking. In the event of a complete stalemate, don't be afraid to leave the final choice to the one who occupies that particular area of responsibility. For example, all other things being considered, the wife should have the final choice on the colour scheme of the kitchen, whilst the husband has the right to choose the final details of the kind of car he will have to drive to work each day; provided neither is being foolishly extravagant!

When you can't agree, just keep talking. Never go running to your parents for their advice; this only creates family divisions. Don't even go to mutual friends; you put them in an impossible situation when they discover that you are asking them to adjudicate! Just keep talking and try to hear what your partner is saying. There was an old Churchillian saying that 'Jaw, Jaw, is better than War, War'. In other words, keep talking and avoid fighting.

Of course cars are more important than toothpaste, and cookers are more important than toilet rolls, but they are still only things after all, and you should never let them become heavy emotional issues. Your partner, and your marriage, are far more important than things. When you have argued yourselves round and round in circles on one of these matters, leave the subject for a few days, or even a few weeks, and then start all over again; try to put out of your minds the prejudices which backed you into a corner before.

Tornadoes (or, babies and bankers)

Beyond the trivialities and the turmoil there are the deep problems that are not solved simply by consulting catalogues and salesmen, or by happy notes left around the house.

For example, what if one partner does not want children, whilst the other does? Our best advice is not to marry until this problem is genuinely sorted out. In fact even if you are agreed that neither of you would like children, it is unwise to get married until you are both prepared to have children if they come. The only certain guarantee of not having children is not to get married.

It is no sin to agree not to have children, but be careful that you do not give your natural affections to other things rather than to people. A word of warning: we have known people who in later years resented their decision not to have children; remember you must live with this decision into old age. Be clear about your motives. If your fear is that children will reduce your standard of living or pleasures, then your motives are rooted in the values of this world.

If you disagree on the number of children you want, be reasonable. Let the wife remember that the husband has to work hard to pay for the children, and let the husband not forget that the wife has to work hard looking after them. If either partner, especially the wife, is afraid of all that is involved in childbirth and child-rearing, then seek counsel together. Talk it over with a valued counsellor. If you are not yet married, don't put it off and say: 'We've got plenty of time to sort that out; we'll talk about it when we are married'. Now is the time.

On the other hand, if you are married and these problems have already arisen, talk openly together and remember that children, whether you plan them or not, are a gift from God and all God's gifts are good. Read Psalm 127 together. Later in this chapter we will have something to say to those who find that they cannot have children.

If you have money problems, the husband should never try to shelter his wife to the point of keeping her in ignorance of mounting debts. That is both dishonest and useless. Work together at solutions. If you cannot make ends meet, don't argue about it and blame each other. Set aside an unhurried evening to go through all the bills. Cut back. There is room for saving in almost every household. Remember, whoever keeps the day-to-day book-keeping, that you are both responsible for the financial security of the home.

Don't argue about finance, because that has never yet paid a debt or saved a pound!

Don't argue about finance, because that has never yet paid a debt or saved a pound! If children come into your family, be especially careful how, when and where you talk over your money problems. Don't keep saying to children, especially young children: 'We can't afford it', or 'We're not made of money you know'. We learnt this lesson the day one of our boys offered us his money box to help us through a difficult patch!

Reacting to disagreements

Go back to question 6 in your assignment. Did you both agree with each others' assessment? Listen carefully to what your partner is telling you at this point.

Have you ever had a 'good row'? You haven't. No rows are good. Avoiding rows is one of the arts of a happy marriage. You will have many debates—and differences! Don't take too much notice of the smiling couple who boast on their golden wedding celebration that they have never had a cross word in their marriage. Only cabbages don't argue! Differences and disagreements you will certainly have, but rows—avoid them like the plague! Rows always lead to irrational anger. Here are five healthy reactions when anger begins to boil in your marriage:

1 See it coming and admit it. Don't be afraid to say 'I'm getting angry; let's stop now'.

2 Make a cup of coffee without further reference to the issue, then sit down and discuss it again; or, if time is short, arrange a specific time later to talk it over.

3 Meet your partner at least half-way by saying: 'Okay, I'm sorry. I'm getting uptight too'. Never respond by cutting in: 'I can see you are getting angry; why don't you just cool down'. That is as effective as trying to quench a fire with petrol.

4 When you lose, admit it.

5 When you win, shut up.

Learn to be a gracious and humble loser. But it is just as important to learn to be a gracious and humble victor. Look for ways of getting your partner off the hook rather than tearing them off a strip.

Most rows are not planned. They are spontaneous combustion; but the fuel may have been leaking into the combustion chamber for a long time.

Concentrate on solutions rather than problems; and concentrate on avoiding arguments rather than winning them. Watch for the things that make your partner angry and then work away quietly to avoid lighting the touch-paper. Aim to understand your partner rather than being understood by him or her. The man who squeals: 'My wife doesn't understand me' has probably been a selfish pig all his life.

Concentrating on solutions rather than problems is so important that we want to give another example, similar to one mentioned earlier. Suppose your husband leaves his dirty clothes lying around the bedroom floor. There are two ways of approaching this problem:

You may say: 'The way you leave your dirty clothes lying around makes this place look like a rubbish tip. What do you think the box in the bathroom is for, storing potatoes in?'

Or you may try: 'I do get a bit uptight about your dirty clothes lying on the bedroom floor. Do you think it will help if we move the washing box into the bedroom?'

Attack the problem, not each other.

Sadly we can be more busy downing our partner than discovering a solution. Never raise your voice and shout at each other; in fact, people only shout because they think no one is listening. If you stop and give your partner a hearing there will be no need to shout. Besides, shouting only obscures clarity. Learn when to switch off the programme. Some rows go on and on and on. Generally, within the first ten minutes or so you have both covered all the relevant points you intend to make.

Proverbs 10:19 'In the multitude of words sin is not lacking, but he who restrains his lips is wise.'

When a husband concludes an argument with, 'Well, I'm boss in this house so you'll just have to do what I say', or a wife with, 'Well, I'll only agree to it if...', you can be sure that this argument will surface again.

The Bible compares a quarrelsome wife to 'a continual dripping on a very rainy day', and adds that restraining her is like restraining the wind or grasping oil with the hand (Proverbs 27:15-16). This is equally true of the disagreeable husband! The partner who is constantly nagging, grumbling, or 'picking a fight', is clearly insecure and unhappy in the marriage. Few things are designed to destroy a marriage more certainly than these.

There are a number of common but unhealthy reactions to differences in a marriage:

1 You can ignore your outburst and pretend you are not angry. But you don't fool anyone that way.

2 You can both try to score points off each other and then each convince yourself you have won. That is the swap-swat kind of argument; it achieves nothing. It's like swatting flies: a lot of energy is used up with very little accuracy and few results.

3 You can go into a silent mood and tell yourself that you are really being self-controlled. In fact you are just feeling sorry for yourself and sulking like a child.

4 You can find secret ways of hurting your partner. At that point you should be asking yourself, 'Is this what love and submission means?'

5 You can exaggerate for effect. But 'always' and 'never' are rarely true.

6 You can let your tongue off the leash. Things said in the heat of the moment can twist a knife and cause a wound that will take years to heal. Unfortunately we all say far too much when we are angry, and then have plenty of time to regret it. James offers us a pretty sad view of the tongue. It's worth reading that description together from James 3:2-12.

...we all say far too much when we are angry, and then have plenty of time to regret it

There are four kinds of animal in the marriage menagerie:

The stubborn mule: 'I'm afraid that's the way I am and you'll just have to get used to it'.

The kicking horse: 'Well, I could start criticising your many faults as well if I had a mind to'.

The biting pony: 'My mother never cooked it that way, and I used to love hers'.

The ungrateful ass: 'Sometimes I wonder why I ever married you'. This is one of the most cruel statements and it should never be heard in your home.

Cross-cultural marriages

In this 'global village' in which we all live, marriages that cross the boundaries of language, race, colour and culture are becoming increasingly common. They are perfectly natural and right. It can be both exciting and fulfilling to blend two cultures, families, and even continents together. You have a wider horizon, and a greater understanding of some of the problems facing the world today—and how to solve them. You certainly have a strong base from which to stand against both racial intolerance and racial hyper-sensitivity. Do be sure to visit and spend time with your partner's family. It is unfair to expect them to travel a long distance to the wedding if you have not had the courtesy to visit them in their home. We would say that it is essential to spend some time, however brief, living in each others' culture. You will learn so much.

However, some of the benefits are mingled with challenges.

Let's take language and culture to start with. The rich experience of sharing with another person their national culture can be offset by the problem of language limitations which means that communication is liable to even more misunderstandings. Children will readily become bilingual, but you may resent the national characteristics of your partner when they dominate in the personality of your children.

These national characteristics must be understood. A cold Anglo-Saxon reserve may find a fiery Latin temperament hard to live with. Don't forget humour, food preferences, and many other things can all be very different. You will both need to respect each other's nationhood, but remember that no one can excuse sin with the claim: 'Oh, that's just my national temperament'. For two Christians, both national culture and citizenship must be placed firmly in submission to Christian culture and the citizenship of the Kingdom of God.

If your marriage crosses the colour bar you must both appreciate the fact that some people can still be very cruel in their looks and conversation; your children may suffer as well. This is not an argument against your marriage but a warning to be ready for reactions.

In these days of wide differences in style and beliefs, even among Christians committed to the authority of the Bible, there are particular problems facing you if you come from a widely different church culture. Worship, church life and organisation, Christian baptism and other doctrines are all areas where a serious division may occur. You **must** talk over these issues now and if you cannot find a meeting of minds you may be incompatible. It should not be on your agenda that you will attend different churches when you are married. Work out what issues are vital to you and what issues are not.

We will assume that it is understood that someone with a committed Christian faith will not marry a partner who has no faith. This can never provide a satisfactory marriage and for this reason Paul writes: 'Do not be unequally yoked together with unbelievers. For what fellowship... has light with darkness?' (2 Corinthians 6:14).

As with so much in this book, there are many more things that could be said about this subject; but we are just seeking to alert you to areas of difference that must be discussed.

Coping with crises

Our plan in this section is not to spoil your cloud nine enjoyment of engagement, or to depress you in the early years of marriage, but to help you face reality and to ask yourselves: 'Is our love strong enough to face together the crises that may occur?' There are many problems that in your future together you will share, but you don't expect them now. Remember our own testimony in chapter one. There is a limit to how far you can even prepare for some of the crises that will occur because they seem to be too remote from your present life together. All we aim to do here is to alert you to some of the situations that may come into your marriage; books have been written on each of these and therefore we have limited ourselves to a few brief comments.

Trials in a deep and strong relationship help to make the bond more firm

Don't adopt the attitude of the world that 'this will never happen to us' because if it does, such a mind-set makes the acceptance of it much harder.

Read through together James 1:2-4. This is why God will bring tests and trials into your marriage. It is certain that he will, the uncertainty is what and when. These trials in a deep and strong relationship help to make the bond more firm. A welder uses heat to make a union strong. That is God's way also. Read 1 Peter 1:6-7.

Illness

If you marry with the knowledge that one or both partners has a health problem, don't be afraid to discuss it together and take wise medical counsel. Discover the possible prognosis and be prepared. However don't become neurotic about it; any marriage can survive ill health, but the problem may be one that will effect you in later years. It may hinder your desire to start a family or it may even interfere with the physical intimacy of your relationship. Be assured that a marriage can be happy and secure without the act of sex, but only if both partners can talk openly together about the challenge of this.

When short-term illness comes into the home, be thoughtful and careful. The husband should remember that if it means that domestic responsibilities fall back to him then that is the meaning of love. When one partner has to attend hospital, go with them. If they are admitted, visit daily and leave behind cards and letters.

By the way, do you know which of you can mop up vomit and diarrhoea? You have a problem if neither of you can do this without adding to it!

Long term illness or disability will pose a threat to any marriage, but there is no reason why it should succeed in destroying it. On the contrary, once both partners have broken through the barrier of frustration, the relationship of love can become deeper and richer. Caring becomes a privilege and time spent together becomes even more enjoyable. There is a difference between fighting against illness and triumphing over it. In the first we refuse to admit its reality and limitations, in the second we build a strong marriage of love and value upon it.

A miscarriage

The Bible has no word for 'foetus'. Both in the Hebrew of the Old Testament and the Greek of the New Testament that which is conceived is referred to as 'a child'. When a woman loses a baby through a miscarriage, however early in pregnancy, it is her child that she has lost; not a foetus or a blob of jelly. She is losing part of herself and it is a bereavement; she therefore needs the loving care and support of her husband who, though feeling the loss, will not feel it in the same intense emotional way. Doctors and nurses can sometimes be thoughtlessly cold and uncaring. Those who are trained to throw unwanted babies into the incinerator are hardly likely to consider a miscarriage as anything more than a minor disappointment. The understanding of a quietly caring husband can mend a mother's aching heart more quickly than anything else.

But there is life beyond a miscarriage. You must both talk together about the future and take medical advice as to how soon it would be wise for you to try again. A young wife may be hesitant in making love for a while.

Bereavement

Remember that the loss of an in-law does not affect you so deeply as it does your partner, however close you may have been. It is *her* mother or *his* father who has died, not yours. Try to enter into the deep sense of loss that they have experienced. When a close relative or friend of your partner dies, don't treat the deceased as if they never existed; talk about them, and don't be afraid to raise the subject and encourage conversation. Make a note of the anniversary of the death so that you are aware of it in following years. Your partner will appreciate your thoughtfulness in this way.

Infertility

Here is a major stress in any family. A wife's longing to be a mother is usually stronger than a husband's longing to be a father. Each month there will be tears as another period comes and goes; every new birth in the church or community will be a painful reminder of what is often felt, quite wrongly, to be a personal failure. Even the dedication or christening of infants in church will be difficult; but to face up to these services rather than avoiding them will strengthen you. Never should the husband coldly order his wife to 'pull yourself together and grow up' when he finds her in tears at the end of the day. Infertility is a hard burden for most women to bear.

If you want a family, don't leave it too long before you start; babies do not always come to order. If you have difficulty starting a family when you want to, don't wait years before you seek medical advice. On the other hand, don't panic after only a few months of trying; and don't blame each other either. If you eventually have to go for tests, the husband must play his part and take the lead. Some husbands assume that it is 'nothing to do with me' and leave it all to their wives to sort out and come up with the answer, but as a matter of fact the problem is likely to be his and not hers. There are many ways in which modern medical science can help childless couples, but we would advise that you give careful thought to some methods used today. If you are offered In Vitro Fertilization (IVF) you must ask searching questions, because your convictions about the sanctity of life from conception may not allow you to accept the deliberate destruction of unwanted fertilised eggs.

Remember that a marriage can be happy and successful without children. Babies may be quite important to you, but they must not be all-important to your marriage.

Post menstrual depression

At the time of a woman's monthly period significant hormonal changes take place and women react to this in different ways. For the great majority the monthly period poses few problems and hardly interferes with the normal pattern of life. However for some the experience of depression, tears and even bizarre behaviour comes with wearisome monthly regularity.

For some women period pain forces them into a day or two of total rest each month. Others experience intense anger, impatience, irritability, touchiness and tears. Sometimes the behaviour of a wife at these times is totally out of character. We have known sweet-natured wives to become so aggressive that even kitchen crockery is not safe!

Before her marriage a woman will already know how she reacts. If she has a negative reaction each month it will quickly become obvious in marriage. It is not helpful to try and conceal the problems before marriage; you will be wise to discuss the subject openly and frankly now. Many men will be quite unaware that a problem like this even exists. If you are already married and the problems are putting significant tension on your relationship you must talk about it. A wife is not alone in facing difficulties each month to one degree or another; many women do. A husband should know the time of the month, watch for the signs, and be sympathetic, thoughtful and understanding. For her part the wife must never trade on her problems or unusual behaviour but must appreciate the pressure this puts on her husband. A healthy diet and good exercise can help, but in extreme cases she should consult her doctor.

As with so many pressures within a marriage, the ability to talk frankly together and with understanding and without recrimination is half-way to resolving the problem.

A handicapped child

This can happen to any family, but there may be more likelihood if you marry older, or if there is a history of congenital disorder in the family. In these days the expectant mother will be offered various tests designed to check whether or not the young child she is carrying is healthy. You need to be aware that often the purpose of the test is not to correct any abnormality, but to destroy a disabled child before birth—with the mother's permission of course! Always ask the purpose of any test before you submit to it; the mother has the right to refuse a test on the ground that she intends keeping her child anyway. Be on your guard also that some tests involve a degree of risk to the unborn child. Let the medical authorities be very clear about your insistence on the value of life from conception. On the other hand, some deficiencies can be corrected if detected in time. Once your views are made known you can generally expect sound advice.

Many couples have been able to see the gift of a handicapped child as a privilege, and not a punishment, and that it was 'according to the purpose of him who works all things according to the counsel of his will' (Ephesians.1:11). There are many books written on this subject today, and you will soon find people who can help, support and advise you. Above all, the responsibilities must be talked through and shared between the husband and the wife. Of course things will not be what you expected them to be, but you can together discover the acceptable will of God.

Redundancy

There is no shame in redundancy and the possibility of it should be shared at once. We found it tragic to hear of a man who said, 'I cannot go home and tell my wife I am out of work; I must find another job first'. Generally a man feels a failure when he is made redundant, and he needs a supporting wife; not a hand-wringing, panicking, weeping woman who whines incessantly: 'How will we pay the bills?' Nor should she be pushing him into any old job just to get him back at work. Constant talking and discussing together is vital.

If there is prolonged unemployment for the husband then it is essential that each day is planned carefully by both husband and wife so that time is used wisely and not wasted. The wife must be particularly sensitive to the husband's feeling of failure, which may lead to despair and depression.

Be warned that sorting out unemployment benefit and various allowances and rebates takes many humiliating interviews, assessments and weeks! A wife needs to be very understanding of how her husband feels. He has not only been declared unwanted at work, but even working in the garden or around the house he may feel guilty that he is not earning his living. On the other hand, a man must not be so fussy about the kind of job he will accept that he virtually keeps himself out of work, nor so comfortable on state support that he does not intend to get employed. If it becomes essential for the wife to get a job, she should never use this fact as a cruel weapon against her husband.

Day One have produced a small booklet on this subject called, *Help! I'm Redundant.*

Depression

Do either of you suffer from depression now? If so, how often, how deeply and for how long?

Discouragement is not depression. A few tears is not depression. A fit of the blues is not depression. The monthly period is not depression either!

Depression is unrelieved unhappiness and unreasonable misery.

Depression is a black cloud of gloom blotting out all positive thoughts.

If either of you suffer from real and deep depression your partner should be aware of this now. Similarly if you are taking anti-depressants, then your partner must know, and you must talk frankly about it.

Any form of mental illness is the most difficult challenge of all in a marriage because it is the one in which you can expect little cooperation from the partner who is ill. You are on your own; it is all one-sided. Every other problem that comes into your marriage you can share together, but you cannot share this one.

However depression, even deep depression, rarely lasts for ever. It will test your marriage bond severely. But it can deepen and strengthen your love. Seek Christian counsel and don't be ashamed to admit depression; it is not a sin.

Some of these crises will certainly come into your home sooner or later. Will your love and commitment be able to stand the test?

A few years ago someone drew our attention to a hymn written by Samuel Medley. We have often quoted it together when circumstances appeared intolerable; it firmly reminded us that God can never make a mistake or act unfairly in our lives. Here are just four of Medley's six verses:

God shall alone the refuge be,
and comfort of my mind;
too wise to be mistaken, he
too good to be unkind.

In all his holy, sovereign will,
He is, I daily find,
too wise to be mistaken, still
too good to be unkind.

What though I can't his goings see,
nor all his footsteps find?
too wise to be mistaken he
too good to be unkind.

Hereafter he will make me know,
and I shall surely find,
he was too wise to err, and O,
too good to be unkind.

Assignment for chapter seven

The intimate life

This assignment should be worked on TOGETHER. *Don't hurry through it, and don't read the chapter until you have completed both the assignment and the Bible study. Find some quiet and leisurely time to complete it.*

1 Will this be the first time you have given serious thought to your future sexual relationship together?

2 Have you been able to discuss this subject together frankly and without embarrassment?

3 Where have you obtained most of your information on this subject?

4 Are you anxious that there may be difficulties in this area of your marriage?

5 If so, have you talked about this seriously together?

6 Can you name three of the most common forms of contraception? And do you know how they are used?

7 Why do you think God created human love-making as the way of propagating the human race ?

8 Many couples have a dissatisfying physical relationship; what reasons do you think could lead to this ?

9 Have either of you had a traumatic or emotionally painful experience of sex in your childhood or life so far?

Bible study for chapter seven

The intimate life

Work though this Bible Study TOGETHER. *Find some quiet and leisurely time for this, and do not attempt to read the chapter until you have completed this study.*

Read Proverbs 5. The whole chapter

The chapter describes the dangers of unfaithfulness in marriage. The passage we will be studying describes the privileges and privacy of love within the home.

Now read verses 15-20 again.

The joy of sexual intimacy is described as 'running water'. In Scripture water is sometimes used as a picture of fullness of joy. Notice how each partner is a spring to refresh the other.

With this in mind:

1 How do you interpret the words in v.15:
'drink'
'your own'?

2 In a sentence what does v.16 mean?

3 Who do you consider the 'strangers' of v.17 to be?

4 Why does v.18 stress 'the wife of your *youth*'?

5 v.19 is a lovely description of the wife. Which three words stand out to you as the most expressive of the ideal relationship between a husband and a wife?

6 v.20 asks the question 'Why?' Can you suggest three reasons why your partner *might be* captivated ('enraptured') by another, and three reasons why they *should not be?*

The intimate life

It is very important that you read this chapter together and in a quiet, unhurried way. But only when you have completed the assignment and Bible study; they are an integral part of the chapter.

HAVE YOU WORKED THROUGH THE ASSIGNMENT AND BIBLE STUDY?

The deepest expression of love

In this chapter we want to be frank and practical in the deepest and most personal area of your married life. Some couples are too embarrassed to speak about this subject with other people. This is understandable, but if you cannot speak about it *together* there will be problems ahead. Many marriages endure an underlying problem and dissatisfaction with the physical relationship, which the husband and wife are never able to solve because neither will talk about it. Your assignment for this chapter, which you worked on together, will either have encouraged you to realise that you can talk freely on this subject or it will have alerted you to your problems of acute embarrassment. We want to raise the subject here in order to overcome that embarrassment if possible. We cannot deal with everything or present much detail; but we shall be as sensitive as possible.

God planned sexual intimacy to be part of the husband and wife relationship. It is a good thing, because God intended it. It is neither accidental nor dirty. Only sin makes us embarrassed about it. Compare Genesis 2:25, where Adam and Eve felt no shame at their nakedness, with Genesis 3:7,10, where they were clearly embarrassed in front of each other and in the sight of God.

According to Hebrews 13:4 marriage is to be held in 'respect' (the word used also means valuable and honourable), and the marriage 'bed' is to be considered pure. In this context the word translated 'bed' is a euphemism for the act of sexual union.

Within marriage the naked body of husband and wife is a perfect fit. God designed each to be 'suitable' for the other (Genesis 2:18 NIV). This is one reason why we know that homosexual relationships are wrong: the two bodies do not fit; they are not 'suitable' for each other and therefore it is not natural.

The sexual union within the loving relationship of a husband and wife is a wonderful gift that brings great joy. There is no deeper way for a husband and wife to be emotionally happy and relaxed than in their physical union together. Locked together in each other's arms the whole world seems good. There is a feeling of 'possessing' your loved one; of an irreversible commitment. Never more clearly will you appreciate the meaning of two becoming one. The physical pleasure is not greater than the emotional and physical contentment. It is God's ultimate in marriage.

The uniqueness of human love-making is intended by God to ensure that children are the result of the deep love and continuing commitment of the parents for one another and not the result of an act of lust.

For your encouragement also, the physical union in marriage is not something to be enjoyed merely in the youthful years of marriage. A loving husband and wife who keep their marriage fresh and alive, may enjoy one another physically into middle age and well beyond. What is more, the early years are not necessarily the best. In a successful marriage there can be a steady improvement in the enjoyment, and the excitement, of the act of 'making love'.

When things go wrong

Let's be frank. It is not unusual for a young couple to find difficulty in achieving the highest joy in sexual intimacy. Like every other area of your marriage this one also has to be worked at.

Be prepared for the possibility that the whole thing may be a let-down in your early weeks or months of marriage. You have waited so long to enjoy one another in this way and you just can't get it right. You long to come to a physical climax together (what is called 'the orgasm'), but perhaps the husband climaxes too soon, or the wife just cannot climax at all. This is nothing to worry about. There must be no accusations: 'It's your fault!' No sense of failure or inadequacy: 'What's wrong with us?' All through your marriage you will not always get it right.

However, don't ignore the problems. Talk about them together. The best time is at once. Immediately after you have made love and something has gone apparently wrong; this is the best time to talk: tenderly, thoughtfully, share the problem together. Never blame your partner. The reason for talking immediately is that it is not an easy subject to bring up 'cold' on some other occasion. It hardly seems appropriate when you are washing the dishes together or weeding the garden!

Remember who you are. Men and women are very different. They are stimulated in a different way. His stimulation is more immediate and physical, hers is more gradual and emotional. She needs to respect him and be loved and wooed by him. These differences are very important to remember.

For this reason the husband must always 'go slowly'. Neither of you are out simply to satisfy your sex urge and get 'a nice feeling'. Your purpose is to show your love, and you want your partner to enjoy your expression of love. A golden rule in making love is: *Always aim to satisfy your partner rather than yourself and in this you will find your own greatest satisfaction.*

Contrary to tradition and gossip, making love, in the fullest sense, is not essential on your first night together. It may not even be either possible or desirable. This is something you must understand beforehand so that there are no unreasonable expectations. Weddings are frequently arranged so far ahead, that it is not always possible for the girl to know exactly what stage of her monthly cycle she will be in on her wedding night. Entering into sex for the first time can be a tense experience; so learn to relax and become familiar with each other's bodies first. Many marriages have been spoilt from the start because after a busy and tiring day intimacy has been entered into in a hurry.

A time to love

Many times an attempt at love-making fails simply because it was not the best time. Something was hindering one partner or both from giving themselves to each other. Here are some common problems:

TIREDNESS

The early months of marriage can be spoilt by late nights whilst you try to get the house in order. You rush home from work, grab a bite of tea, do some necessary housework, and then there's a long hard slog stripping walls, making good the plaster, hanging paper, painting and so on. At midnight you fall exhausted into bed. If this continues, sometimes night after night, week after week, it is little wonder that both partners become frustrated and irritable.

Sometimes the young husband is working hard at his profession or job, and maybe studying hard in the evenings as well. When eventually he gets to bed, he is dog-tired and falls asleep at once. His young wife, on the other hand, is all ready and waiting for him. Ten years later the roles are reversed. He has arrived and is on top of his work. He is all ready. She is now harassed by housework and three lively children. She falls asleep as soon as she drops into bed.

In either case there are two possible solutions. The first is to plan your week more sensibly. Neither the house nor a career is more important than a marriage. You must plan for that evening together that we spoke about in chapter three. But the biggest failure may be to assume that making love has to be done last thing at night! There are many other times when it is more appropriate and more enjoyable. Be imaginative! But whatever you do, try to avoid getting over tired for long periods.

WORRY

It is hard to relax in mind and body if one partner is anxious and troubled about matters at work, at home or even at church; or with parents, in-laws, finance or health. All that we have said on the subject of communication should help us here. A wife can lovingly lift a husband's worry; sometimes she will need to woo him if he is discouraged or anxious about his work. A wife who admires her husband, and tells and shows him so, will do wonders for his self-confidence. It may be that it is the wife who is anxious about something; she is longing for a sympathetic listener, not merely a husband who wants to 'make love'. Gently talking about the problems can lead to a deep expression of caring.

EMBARRASSMENT

Some couples go through their entire married life making love under the duvet with the lights off! This may well reveal a deep-seated embarrassment about the whole subject. But there is nothing to hide. It is not a deed necessarily done in the dark. Why not make a point right from the beginning of your life together of keeping the lights on. This will do wonders for your confidence together and in helping you to overcome your embarrassment.

A LACK OF ROMANCE

A good marriage doesn't have sex, it has romance. There is a world of difference. A prostitute and her client, the promiscuous fellow and girl, the one night stand, and the casual acquaintance are all examples of just sex. It is animal behaviour, destroying human dignity. Intimacy within marriage is a different world of relationship. It springs out of a deep, constant love, a total commitment and mutual trust, and a high regard and respect for the one you married. But if you are no longer excited at the prospect of your partner then something is certainly going wrong. Wake up to the fact that romance is slipping out of your marriage. Something must be done to correct this, and it must be done quickly.

Have you both become drab and unattractive to each other? Are you taking each other for granted? Has someone else slipped into your relationship? Try to identify why you no longer excite each other, why you no longer look into each other's face, eye to eye. Take action.

A WIFE'S PROBLEMS

There are some problems in a marriage that are carried only by the wife. Sometimes she experiences a coldness, a frigidity that makes it impossible for her to enjoy her husband; as a result the whole relationship becomes a drag to her. She may not even be sure what the cause is; this is where some frank but gentle talking is necessary, and perhaps even some professional counselling.

A young wife may be afraid of becoming pregnant. It would never occur to the husband, but after the act of intercourse, whatever the precautions, a wife often contemplates the possibility of a pregnancy. Perhaps she is afraid that a pregnancy would spoil their financial plans, or that the husband would not want a baby yet. She may even be afraid of carrying and giving birth to a child, or she may feel that she could never cope with looking after it. These are all very natural fears, and if only she will talk to him about it, her husband can go a long way to reassure his wife on every count. If he fails, then a wise counsellor, whether a doctor, family planning counsellor or wise and trusted friend may be able to help. Incidentally, if a girl is afraid of conceiving, carrying or caring for a child, she must seek out some help before she gets married. It is no use dismissing these fears with a careless: 'Oh, it'll be all right once I'm married'. It may be, but not necessarily.

Another cause for a wife's frigidity may be that her husband takes too little concern to prepare his wife before intercourse. Perhaps there is no love-making, no romance beforehand. He thinks she 'turns on' and is ready just as quickly as he is. Never forget that a wife can be forced by her husband. Sadly, many are. The law goes even further and claims that a wife can be raped by her husband. If a husband is rough, or insists on union before the wife is ready, or perhaps demands an approach to intercourse that the wife finds objectionable and unnatural then the whole experience can be very painful for her. The next time she will be thinking of the pain or humiliation and will be unable to give herself freely to her husband.

In this area of life, as in every area for the Christian, there are some things practised by the world that will instinctively be felt to be wrong and degrading for those who are committed to Christ. We are not expected to follow a fallen world. A husband who insists on making love at a time when it is simply unpleasant, or in a manner that the wife finds humiliating, must not be surprised if she freezes whenever he makes an approach to her.

Some of you who are reading this may have come to Christ, and then to marriage, out of a promiscuous way of life; all that must be abandoned in thought as well as in actions, because compassion and tenderness, selflessness and love are the new Christian values for physical intimacy.

Remember our golden rule in making love: *Always aim to satisfy your partner rather than yourself, and in this you will find your own greatest satisfaction.*

Every man and woman is different. A wife's coldness need not be a disaster providing she can think through the reasons and share them openly with her husband.

Paul has a very practical approach to this area of marriage in 1 Corinthians 7:3-5. Open your Bible and read these verses together. You will see that both the husband and the wife must remember that each has a responsibility to satisfy the other partner and be 'available'. But at the same time, each partner must be sensitive to the limitations that may be imposed by health, anxiety, or as Paul implies here, even a time of spiritual devotion.

A PARTNER'S PREVIOUS EXPERIENCE

The final question of your assignment may have proved to be the most sensitive, and even the most hurtful of all. In these tragic days of pre-Christian promiscuity, child abuse, rape, and even the results of Christians backsliding, it is wise for a partner to share such an experience with the one they intend to marry. A marriage doesn't get off to a good start with significant undisclosed skeletons in the cupboard. The assignment question may have opened up an issue you had been trying hard to forget; but don't be afraid of it. If your partner really loves you, such an admission will be met with a loving and reassuring response. Sadly, a traumatic experience like those we have just mentioned, can leave scars that will reappear exactly when you least want them to. At the moment of making love in your marriage all the old horror may resurface. If you can talk about this with your partner and, if you both feel the need, with a Christian counsellor as well, then you should find no difficulty in your future.

How then?

CHOOSE YOUR TIME

As we have already indicated, love-making does not have to be at night. Daytime is easy for a young couple without the ties of a family. Going to bed early or making love in the morning, or for that matter at any other time, is just as appropriate. The husband should make it his business to know the time of his wife's monthly period and avoid making advances when he knows it would be distasteful for both of them. Similarly he should be considerate over her tiredness or lack of response. 1 Peter 3:7 is just as relevant here as anywhere, 'Husbands, dwell with (your wives) with understanding'. Self-control is a Christian virtue that every husband needs.

CHOOSE YOUR PLACE

Many couples when they get married and step into their new home set about redecorating the lounge to their exact taste. All their spare money goes into the decorations and furnishings of this 'show piece'. Then, and only then, they are ready to entertain their friends. This is mistake number one. The first room to be decorated in your new home should be your bedroom; and the choice of decor belongs to the wife. In the bedroom the lighting and fittings should be as romantic as possible. The tragedy is that once you leave aside the bedroom it comes very low on the list of priorities; it may be ten years or more before you ever get round to sorting it out. So, our serious advice is that you decorate the bedroom first. It is even more important than the kitchen—which comes second. Until those two rooms are complete, let your friends sit on boxes as they initial the tatty wallpaper in the lounge!

PAY ATTENTION TO PERSONAL HYGIENE

It is very hard to make romantic love to bad breath and smelly armpits! Personal hygiene means taking regular showers and keeping your clothes fresh; pay attention to body odour and bad breath. Spray on some perfume, splash on a bit of after-shave, make yourself attractive to your partner. Just as you want your partner to be attractive to you.

LOVE COMES FROM LIFE

You can't expect to have a satisfying intimate life if you spend all day hurting each other. A strong leader-husband who loves his wife and studies her needs, seeing how he can please her, will certainly find a wife ready for his advances. Similarly, a wife who is loving and caring, submissive to his leadership and taking care over her appearance, will not find a husband lacking in his attentions to her.

When not to

Never force your partner, either physically, emotionally or psychologically—'If you love me you will'—when he or she is clearly not in the mood and is unable or unwilling to respond to your advances.

Never make love as a solution to an unresolved argument. Don't think you can have a row in the kitchen and solve it in the bedroom. Settle it in the kitchen and you can seal it in the bedroom.

Never make love merely to relieve tension or to selfishly 'enjoy sex'. If you ever find yourself making love with someone *else* in mind then something is going terribly wrong; this is an alarm signal.

In other words your love-making must be an expression of your desire for the one you married and if anyone else would do then you are missing the whole point. Making love is an expression of what words cannot say; it is God's way of helping even the most un-poetic amongst us tell our loved one how we really feel about them.

Keeping love in your home

What we have just said leads us very naturally into one of the most important areas of your life together. Stop right here for a moment and read together Proverbs 5:15-20. You should have already completed your Bible Study together so, when you have read the passage in Proverbs, just look through your answers to the study. Now read on.

Increasingly, Christian marriages are breaking up and Christian ministers are spending more time in marriage counselling with their own members than ever before. Your marriage will be under attack right from the beginning. Remember: 'The heart is deceitful above all things, and desperately wicked;

who can know it?' (Jeremiah 17:9). Never convince yourself that your marriage is too safe. It isn't. There are at least four pressures that the devil will be using to prise your love apart.

THE PRESSURE OF THE WORLD

Britain leads Europe in the divorce rate, with three out of five marriages ending in the divorce courts; the standards and expectations of the world are getting lower every year. The moral squeeze of the media is convincing couples that it is all quite natural to be unfaithful or simply to live together. You are facing a major task to keep your 'marriage bed pure' (Hebrews 13:4 NIV).

The world generally places a low value on the importance of faithfulness to the marriage vows. Some years ago we heard a programme on the radio in which it was claimed: 'The wife who does not flirt grows old prematurely; the husband who has no affairs loses confidence in himself'. Since this is the attitude of many, we were not surprised to read the advertisement: 'Isn't it time you flirted with your wife, other men do'. There is no place for the Christian to flirt with anyone, it is all part of what the Bible plainly calls 'The lust of the flesh' (1 John 2:16). Magazines, television, the press and the radio are all telling you how to run your life. The Christian has only one reliable guide.

In our lustful society where God's pattern is generally ignored, people are advocating 'open marriages'. This means that, providing both partners agree and are kept informed, each should be free to have as many extra-marital affairs as they want. Whatever the media may say, this will ultimately bring only misery to a family and a society. God's pattern is plain and is a recipe for security: 'Because of sexual immorality, let each man have his own wife, and let each woman have her own husband' (1 Corinthians 7:2).

THE PRESSURE OF YOUR OWN FANTASY

Watching or listening to 'soaps', reading romantic novels, allowing your mind to wander whilst you are ironing or fixing the car. All these fantasies impress you with the thought: 'I want my life to be like that'. This is a special danger for the wife at home. Many young wives, harassed by housework, tied by a family, and bogged down with a marriage that is running into the doldrums, live high on fantasies. Too many afternoon 'soaps', radio plays, or short stories can be a curse to your marriage. Philippians 4:8 will help you here: 'Whatever things are true, whatever things are noble, whatever things are just, whatever things are pure, whatever things are lovely, whatever things are of good report, if there is any virtue, and if there is anything praiseworthy—meditate on these things'. And if this does not work, try Matthew 5:27-30. Looks can kill your marriage. Once you detect the snare, get rid of it.

THE PRESSURE OF YOUR ENVIRONMENT

The girls in the office, or sadly even at church, often dress in a way that is calculated to turn men on. And the young wife should realise that she can lead others into sin by being too low at the neck or too high at the hem, or just too flimsy everywhere; the only person you need to impress is your husband because your body is his alone. A young husband should not encourage his wife to wear revealing or provocative clothes—if he values her.

The advertising hoardings, the conversations among the people you work with, even the stickers in the rear windows of cars, are all pressures to make you think and feel in the mould of the world. Sin has been made to look very attractive, 'She says to him' "Stolen water is sweet, and bread eaten in secret is pleasant". But he does not know that the dead are there' (Proverbs 9:17-18). To give in to the pressure of those around you, even for one moment, can be the death of your marriage.

Never say: 'Our marriage is too secure, our love is too deep, our self-control is too strong'

THE PRESSURE OF PROBLEMS IN YOUR MARRIAGE

Many things can force a partner out of the home and into the arms of someone else: a dissatisfying physical relationship, a husband who ceases to take the lead in the marriage, a wife who becomes frumpish and drab, rows over petty differences, or a nagging partner who will never leave the other one alone, jealousy and over-protectiveness. Never say: 'Our marriage is too secure, our love is too deep, our self-control is too strong'. You are fooling yourselves. 'If you think you are standing firm, be careful that you don't fall!' (I Corinthians 10:12 NIV).

Turn together to Hebrews 13:4 'Marriage should be honoured by all, and the marriage bed kept pure, for God will judge the adulterer and all the sexually immoral' (NIV). And remember that little word in 1 Peter 3:1 'Wives be submissive to **your own** husbands'. In your Bible study together, what did you make of question 4? Notice it is the wife 'of your youth' not 'in your youth'. That is a significant difference. A husband should never 'use' his wife in her beauty and abandon her in middle age. Your love for each other and your enjoyment of each other's company, can grow more, not less, with advancing years.

Watch for the signs

Be alert to any and every indication that you are misusing your marriage.

THE SECOND LOOK

When you see someone who attracts you, 'Do not lust after her beauty in your heart nor let her allure you with her eyelids' (Proverbs 6:25). Move away at once and repeat to yourself Job 31:1, 'I have made a covenant with my eyes; why then should I look upon a young woman?' These verses apply equally to the wife.

THE FLUTTERING HEART

You know how your heart flutters now at the approach of your partner? You only have to hear that voice or those footsteps, or even the roar of his Honda 500 and you know what happens! The alarm bells should ring whenever the same occurs over someone else. 'Keep your heart with all diligence, for out of it spring the issues of life' (Proverbs 4:23).

THE ARRANGED MEETING

We are not referring only to the deliberate appointment, but the subconscious excuse for working in her office today, or sitting with him in church this evening; even passing the same shop or house because there is someone by whom you want to be noticed. You can be certain others are noticing as well! Remember, 'The ways of man are before the eyes of the Lord' (Proverbs 5:21).

THE EXCUSE FOR A CHAT

The long phone calls that you pretend to yourself are necessary for business. Come off a committee if you are too much enjoying the conversation you have with another member. Never take a member of the opposite sex to their home in your car and sit outside chatting. If you *must* take them home, drop them off quickly and tell your husband or wife who you dropped home this evening. 'Remove your way far from her, and do not go near the door of her house.' (Proverbs 5:8).

THE MENTAL COMPARISON

Convincing yourself that the other person is better than your partner. It is all the excitement of forbidden fruit. 'Do not lust after her beauty' (Proverbs 6:25).

THE SEXUAL LONGING

When the sight of someone else hits you in the stomach remember, 'Can a man take fire to his bosom, and his clothes not be burned' (Proverbs 6:27).

THE FLATTERING ATTENTION

When another person speaks often with you and compliments you, it may be wonderful for your ego, but it is disastrous for your marriage. One compliment is acceptable, the second is a warning light, 'The lips of an immoral woman drip honey, and her mouth is smoother than oil' (Proverbs 5:3).

What do you do?

FIRST OF ALL, THINK!

What is happening to your marriage? What are you doing to your marriage partner and your marriage vows? What will become of your Christian testimony and what will the world think of your Saviour, Jesus Christ? Your marriage is under attack, so run away from the temptation before it becomes irresistible. Remember the godly example of Joseph in the house of Potiphar. Read together Genesis 39:7-15, and don't forget that Joseph was not even married at this time; but he treated everyone's marriage as private property. Remember also what God said to Abimelech when he thought of taking Abraham's wife, Sarah, as his own wife, even though Abimelech was unaware that she was married, 'You are a dead man because of the woman whom you have taken, for she is a man's wife' (Genesis 20:3). That is what God thinks about adultery.

If you are married and already have children, what will your unfaithfulness do to them? Research shows that children from broken homes are scarred for life, and their own marriage is more likely to fail. And what will they think of you?

Why ruin your life and that of your family for the passing pleasure of a moment's sin?

THEN, DON'T THINK

Whenever that person comes into your mind, firmly change the subject. Remember that all thoughts are merely the seed-bed for action. And wrong thoughts are sin. In Matthew 15:19 our Lord shows us the progression that leads to sinful actions:

First the heart: I want

Then the mind (thoughts): I will

Finally the action: I do

That's the way it goes. So when your evil longings reach the mind and you start entertaining them and scheming, they are already half way to action.

DON'T LOOK

Look the other way. Turn to Proverbs 6:25 and Job 31:1 if you cannot recall them from earlier. You must discipline yourself to look away before the temptation becomes irresistible. Looks can kill your marriage.

DON'T TOUCH

Hands off! Hugging and kissing other people is a curse to a marriage. Reserve your hugs and kisses for your own wife or husband alone. We would put a three line whip on that, even though it is contrary to the current fashion in many Christian circles. There is far too much easy touch among Christians today; and that is just one reason why many Christian marriages are coming unstuck.

DON'T TALK

If you know there is a problem arising then avoid that person. In addition to what we said earlier about giving other people a lift home, a husband or wife would be very unwise to entertain a member of the opposite sex in the home when they are alone. A third person must always be with you. We would encourage you to start that arrangement immediately.

DON'T GIVE UP ON YOUR OWN MARRIAGE

All marriages will get a bit 'down at heel' from time to time. Put some sparkle back into your own marriage. Arrange a surprise weekend away, buy a special and unexpected gift, or at least redecorate the bedroom! Work at keeping each other. Head off the opposition by being constantly attractive to your partner in loving care and in neat appearance. The husband or wife who comes home from work hot and tired should immediately wash and change. Similarly, a wife at home is well advised to change neatly before her husband arrives. Little gifts, warm greetings, plenty of verbal appreciation. All these help to preserve your own marriage. Don't ever take each other for granted.

When do you share?

If you discover you have wrong feelings towards another person, do you share this with your marriage partner immediately? The answer is definitely, No. Handle it first on your own; asking God's help and wisdom but not forgetting that the largest part is sheer common sense, self discipline, and a determination to make your marriage work. If you talk too soon to your partner you may simply destabilise your relationship by creating suspicion and mistrust.

It is a different matter if you discover that another person has a crush on you that annoys you. Handle it firmly on your own at first, and if you are not succeeding in cutting them off, ask your partner for help and support. Assure your marriage partner of your love and explain how annoying this attention from 'outside' is to you. Work at it together.

What if you see someone paying attention to your marriage partner? Gently draw it to your partner's attention and talk about the ways of helping and avoiding it. If they get annoyed at having this drawn to their attention, then perhaps they have something to feel guilty about.

In flesh and spirit they are his

Before you leave this section, read together Malachi 2:13-16. Notice that the Lord is watching your marriage, you are partners and have entered into a marriage covenant. Notice again the reference to 'the wife of your youth'. But not only this, your union in marriage makes you one in body and spirit, and both belong to the Lord. So 'Take heed to your spirit' if you want to guard your union and if you want to safeguard your offspring. Two into one will go.

Family planning

We are grateful in this section to Dr John Beale, a General Practitioner for more than thirty years, for his advice on birth control methods; however, all views and judgements expressed are our own.

A loving and caring relationship .. will take you a long way together

The techniques of love-making are something that a couple should learn from each other, rather than from a book. The 'I want to experience it all now' approach is not a happy one for a marriage. Part of the excitement of your sexual relationship will be growing together; to read it all from a book before you have begun is rather like reading the last chapter of an exciting story before the first! A loving and caring relationship in which the principles we have offered are understood, and the golden rule is applied, will take you a long way together: *Always aim to satisfy your partner rather than yourself, and in this you will find your greatest satisfaction.*

Very few couples will have such serious problems with their sexual life that they will need to consult a doctor. However, a doctor's advice regarding contraception can be important and you may wish to consult your family doctor or family planning clinic a couple of months before your wedding in order to get up-to-date advice from someone who is trained to deal with this important matter. Go together; this is not a subject that should be left just to the young girl to decide.

Some Christian couples feel a little uneasy about the whole question of birth-control. Somehow they feel that it may be interfering with God's right to give us children, and anyway, it is unnatural. Of course there is no compelling reason why you may not choose to leave the whole matter in God's hands and refuse all forms of family planning. But you must be prepared to take the consequences of this if children come at inconvenient times or in inappropriate numbers! However, there is no biblical reason to forbid birth-control. Whilst God has forbidden us the right to terminate the life of others, he has allowed us the right to make reasonable decisions about when a life should begin. We must be responsible to society and to each other.

Some Christians are troubled that by exercising birth control they may be violating the command of God to Adam and Eve that they should 'Be fruitful and multiply; fill the earth and subdue it' (Genesis 1:28); this was repeated to Noah and his family in Genesis 9:1. The judgement of God upon Onan, who practised withdrawal (known as *coitus interruptus*) and 'spilled his seed on the ground' rather than give a child to his brother's widow, is often taken as a severe warning against any form of birth control (Genesis 38:9 NIV).

However, we have no reason to assume that God's command to Adam and Noah was intended as an order to every couple for all time. Humanity has adequately fulfilled the Creator's plan to populate the world, and caring for our resources is one good reason for birth control. Onan, on the other hand, was in conflict with an ancient law that would later be reinforced in Deuteronomy 25:5-6. The sin was in his selfish motive of denying a male heir to his deceased brother, and not in the action of preventing conception as such. The key is found in the phrase, 'Onan knew that the heir would not be his' (v.9).

The Bible makes no explicit judgement against birth control, which it surely would if such action was sinful. Birth control for reasons of social responsibility, the health of the mother, or for spiritual duties (see 1 Corinthians 7:5) either by abstinence or intervention, does not appear to contradict the teaching of the Bible. Equally, those who prefer to use no form of birth control have a perfect right to their conviction.

Of course it is possible simply to abstain from making love during the wife's most fertile period each month. This 'fertility awareness' approach is practised by many. But it is not reliable as a method on its own. Besides, it is a form of birth-control anyway, and why should your deep expression of love be reduced to a few 'safe' days each month? Similarly, from a practical viewpoint Onan's example is not recommended. For the husband to withdraw just before the ejaculation of sperm is frustratingly unsatisfying for both partners, and almost certain to result in a conception sooner or later since only one seed from the many millions produced by the man is required for conception.

In order to prepare yourselves for that possible consultation with your family doctor, we shall mention the most commonly used, and easily obtained, methods of contraception.

THE CONTRACEPTIVE PILL

This is taken regularly by the woman and acts by preventing ovulation taking place. If the woman's eggs are not released by the ovaries (ovulation), they obviously cannot be fertilized. The method is very popular and used commonly by newly weds. It is an effective method providing you carefully follow the instructions enclosed with the tablets. The 'pill' can be used to delay a period so that it does not coincide with an important event such as the wedding day! Hence the reason for consulting your doctor or family planning clinic some months before your wedding.

Whilst the value of the pill is that it in no way interferes with the spontaneity of love-making, there are significant potential dangers in it. If you read carefully the warning that is enclosed with them of possible side-effects, you will see what we mean. The dangers are statistically slight, but you must consult your doctor to determine whether or not the pill is safe for you, and if he considers it may endanger your health, he will not prescribe it. The pill is only obtainable on a doctor's prescription and he will want to check on you from time to time. You must weigh up the health risks involved.

You should be aware of the fact that the so-called 'morning after' pill works differently, and is used by some doctors to abort any fertilized egg after unprotected intercourse; it is referred to as an 'abortifacient.' The Bible has no word for 'foetus' or 'embryo' and the same word for the young child of Isaiah 9:6 is used also of the child in the womb in Exodus 21:22. The same is true in the New Testament; compare Luke 1:41 and 2 Timothy 3:15. Life begins at conception and we must therefore treat the newly conceived baby with the full dignity of humanity.

BARRIER METHODS

These methods simply stop the sperm reaching the egg so that fertilization cannot take place.

THE CAP

Sometimes referred to as the 'diaphragm', this is inserted into the vagina and it covers the entrance to the womb (uterus). Initially this should be fitted by a doctor or nurse, but subsequently it is easily managed by the woman herself. The cap can interrupt the spontaneity of love-making unless it is fitted well beforehand.

THE SHEATH, OR CONDOM.

This rubber sheath is slipped over the erect penis prior to its entry into the vagina. Inevitably this method does interrupt the act of making love; however it is widely used and can even become part of the love-making.

Both these barrier methods should be used in conjunction with a spermicide foam, cream or gel which is easy to use and can be prescribed by a doctor or bought at most chemists. When a barrier method of contraception is used with a spermicide, unplanned pregnancies are not common.

THE INTRA UTERINE DEVICE

The IUD, or 'coil' as it is often known, is a foreign body placed in the uterine cavity to stop a fertilized egg implanting itself in the lining of the uterus. The IUD can be left in the uterus for long periods of time but it must be placed by a doctor and it needs to be checked regularly. The IUD is falling from favour as a contraceptive device chiefly because it has caused various health complications. In addition to this, for those who believe that life begins at the moment of conception the IUD is seen as causing an abortion since it operates to cancel an already fertilized egg.

STERILIZATION

When a couple are sure that they should have no more children, for whatever reason, the ultimate form of limiting family size is sterilization. This is achieved by simple operations which tie off the tubes leading, in the woman, from the ovary to the womb, or in the man, from the testes to the urethra. Your family doctor can arrange this operation. The simplest operation is that on the man (a vasectomy), and even if done privately is not very expensive.

Both partners should realise that for all practical purposes this is an irreversible step. Reversal operations are not often successful. Only in exceptional circumstances, therefore, is sterilization appropriate for a newly married couple. Even if you have both agreed that you do not want children, we would strongly advise against sterilization; a few years of marriage often changes your attitude towards having a family.

Finally you need to remember that no system of birth control is one hundred per cent reliable and all who marry should be prepared for a pregnancy and the joys and trials of welcoming children into the world.

There are other methods of contraception that you can discuss with your doctor or family planning clinic but be sure that they explain any risks involved; and for your part you must make clear that you do not want any form of contraception that involves an abortion of a fertilized egg. The value of life from the moment of conception is too precious to be traded for an easy solution to an unwanted pregnancy.

Planning your wedding

This chapter is designed for those who are engaged to be married and who, sooner or later, will be fixing a date for the wedding. Until you decide on the actual day there is not too much detailed planning that you can do, though you can dream! Once you have announced the date suddenly everything takes off. There is a lot to do, but don't panic, you will get it all done even though at times you begin to despair. Take encouragement from the fact that all young couples have felt the same and yet they somehow got everything ready on time. You will be no exception.

The purpose of this chapter is simply to draw your attention to some of the things that you need to start working on right away. We offer as much help as we think is necessary and make a few suggestions from our experience of being involved with many engaged couples for three decades. However, traditions and customs are constantly changing, and you must not hold us responsible for anything we suggest that may prove to be misleading! Take or discard whatever you want from this chapter and the next. Your parents may find some value in reading these two chapters also!

Let's start from the beginning and take things in order.

The date and preparing your budget

It will be advisable not to decide on a date that is too close. It may sound all very exciting to set a date just two months ahead, but unless you are both planning to take two months off work you will soon regret your impatience.

You will have all kinds of reasons why a particular date is a favourite for you both. Perhaps it will be close to one of your birthdays, the anniversary of your engagement, or it may be just a convenient date. The first thing to do is to discuss the date with your parents and then, if you already know who your Best Man and Bridesmaids will be, give them a phone call to check that they are free. Then contact the minister, vicar or other Christian leader to book the date at the church. But be careful, you could go on checking with so many people that you will never find a suitable day.

Now you will need to prepare a budget. Weddings are very expensive things and there is no such thing as a wedding 'on the cheap', unless you are going to have a small family affair with no friends, flowers or wedding dress! Most couples want their wedding day to be something very special. However, don't borrow to fund your wedding because you should never borrow to finance a depreciating asset. A marriage lasts for a life time, a wedding usually lasts around eight hours.

To start with, you will have little idea of costs, but a few phone calls to friends and the professionals will give you some figures to put down. Always over estimate. You must start with this budget planning or you will suddenly find you have dreams of a wedding you cannot possibly afford. Here are the main items that must be included:

★ **The reception** (hall or hotel, food, drink and cake). Traditionally this is the responsibility of the Bride's parents, but it is increasingly common for everyone to 'pitch in'. Very early on, sort out who will pay for what and write a note to everyone concerned to confirm these financial arrangements; this may save a lot of embarrassment later.

★ **Your honeymoon.** Absolutely essential!

★ **Dresses** for the Bride and Bridesmaids and any Pageboys.

★ **A suit** for the Groom.

★ **Going-away clothes.**

★ **Flowers** for the church and reception.

★ **Bouquets** for the Bride and Bridesmaids. (The Groom's responsibility).

★ **Small gifts** for the Best Man, Bridesmaids and other friends to whom you wish to express your appreciation for their help on your day.

★ **Church, minister's, choir and bell-ringers' fees,** where applicable.

★ **Registration fees.**

★ **Cars.** Hire fees are greatly inflated for weddings, so find out the cost for a 'function' before you reveal that it is a wedding – and spot the difference.

★ **Photographer.**

★ **And don't forget the rings!**

Don't panic when you see the result. There are always ways in which you can ease the cost here and there.

The law and your wedding

Bringing the law into your wedding day may sound threatening, but your marriage is not just a private affair between you and a few friends and relatives. Marriage is a social contract, which means that society takes an interest and not only makes sure you are properly married but that you intend to stay that way. Every marriage in the United Kingdom has to be registered and conducted in a proper way for it to be recognised according to the laws of this country.

Marriage is not just a private affair ... it is a social contract

There is a difference in the way the legal aspects of your marriage are dealt with in the Free Churches (including the Roman Catholic Church) in England and Wales, in the Church of England, and in Scotland, so we will take them in that order.

The following details, including the vows that you must make, are correct at the time of this book going to press; however, there are proposals before the government that may change a number of areas, particularly that relating to the licensing. Many factors such as a divorce, brief residence in the country, or different parishes, registration districts or country of residence, can affect the procedure. If in doubt over anything, ask the Registrar for advice—and ask in plenty of time.

The Free Church marriage in England and Wales

The first thing to do is to go to your minister or appropriate church leader to clear the date, asking whether the church has an Authorised Person to act on behalf of the Registrar at your wedding. This is generally the minister himself, or one of the church officers. If the answer is positive then you do not require an outside Registrar to be present at the marriage. If the church does not have an Authorised Person, you will need to have a Registrar present.

Your next step—whether or not your church has its own Authorised Person—is to visit your local Register Office. They are prepared to take provisional booking of a marriage up to twelve months in advance. As the law currently stands, you must give notice at least twenty-two days before the date of your proposed marriage. You can find the address of your local Register Office in the telephone directory under: 'Registration of Births, Marriages and Deaths'; look down until you find your district under 'Marriage (Superintendent Registrars)'. If you don't know which district you are in then phone any of the numbers and they will tell you.

You can go to the office at any time during their normal working hours, but you should phone to make an appointment first; few offices will see you on a Saturday. Both of you should attend, preferably together, and be sure to take with you a current passport or birth certificate for each of you. Simply explain that you want to get married on such and such a date. If your church has an Authorised Person you are applying for a 'Superintendent's Certificate for Marriage'. Without this your minister cannot conduct the marriage. If either of you has been through a form of marriage before, in this or any other country, you will need to provide documentary evidence that the marriage has ended.

Unless you are in a great hurry to get married, your marriage will be by certificate without a licence. The Superintendent Registrar will enter on an official form the details you give him, such as names, ages, addresses, and place of marriage. A copy of this form will be displayed on the notice board at the Register Office for twenty-one days, and if no objection has been made by the end of this time, then he can issue the certificate. When you have this certificate, take it to your minister or the Authorised Person immediately. That is your contact with the Register Office finished.

This three weeks' public notification can be significantly shortened (at a price) by obtaining a superintendent's certificate *and licence*. Again the Superintendent Registrar will enter your details on a form which is not posted on the public notice board but is entered into the licence notice book. Only one full working day has to pass before the certificate and licence can be issued.

Your certificate is valid for twelve months, so you can apply for it some time before your wedding date. We would advise that you do not apply much earlier than eight or nine months prior, so that the certificate will run well past your proposed wedding date—just in case you have to postpone your day for health or other reasons.

If your church does not have an Authorised Person, which means that you will need to have an official Registrar in attendance, the Register Office will not consider your application more than three months ahead of the date. Naturally there is an extra charge for having a Registrar in attendance, and this must be paid to the Registrar by the Best Man on the day of the wedding. He should have the exact amount in a sealed envelope. For your own peace of mind you may like to telephone the office a week before your wedding to check that they have you in their diary. They are busy people but they will thank you for the phone call, and you will all sleep more easily afterwards.

Providing both of you have been living in the same registration district for at least seven days prior to you going to the Registrar then you need only go to the one office. If you both live in different areas then you must each go to the office in your own area. Check this out and don't assume you are in the same district just because you live near each other; boundaries have to be drawn somewhere and it may be at the end of your road.

A marriage can take place in a building other than those traditionally registered 'for the solemnizing of marriages'. However, this does not mean *any* building. There are two important points to note: First, the building must be 'seemly and dignified' as a place for the solemnizing of marriages and as such it must be approved by the local authority. Your local Register Office will hold a list of such buildings; they are known as 'Approved Premises'. Secondly, only a civil ceremony can take place in such a building. Therefore a religious ceremony can only take place in a building registered for the solemnizing of marriages. A marriage cannot take place before 8.00 am or after 6.00 pm.

If you wish to have a wedding ceremony in a building that is neither registered for the solemnization of marriages nor on the list of Approved Premises you can—*but it will not be a legal marriage ceremony*. It is not uncommon for a couple to arrange to be legally married in their local Register Office the day prior to their Christian ceremony in the building of their choice. A marriage in a civil Register Office must be non-religious. As a matter of fact, you can be married by a civil ceremony in any Register Office or Approved Premises in

England and Wales; it does not have to be in the registration district in which either of you live. In this case you will make your appointment with the Register Office where you wish to marry, but give notice of marriage at your local Office, following the procedure outlined above.

If you are still in any doubt about your situation then the local Register Office will be only too pleased to help you. Don't be afraid to ask the Registrar; they are there to advise you. Don't rely on your friends who, with the best intention, may give you wrong information.

A marriage in the Church of England in England and Wales

Your first step is to contact the vicar (who may be known by another title, like 'Rector' or 'Minister in Charge') in whose church you wish to get married, in order to clear the date you have in mind. He may ask you to attend marriage preparation classes. In the Church of England you do not deal with the local Register Office directly. Normally in the Church of England you can be married only in the church of the parish where one of you lives or in a church where one of you is on the church Electoral Roll.

On three Sundays prior to your marriage your 'banns' must be read. This means your intention to marry will be read out at public worship on each of those Sundays. This must be done between three months and twenty-two days (i.e. three Sundays) before the wedding. There is no legal obligation for either of you to be present to hear your banns being read, but many couples make a point of attending at least once; the minister will often include prayers for those soon to be married.

It may be that either the Bride or the Groom lives outside the parish in which the marriage is to take place. In this case the party concerned, let's say the Groom, must contact the vicar of his own parish because the banns must be read in that parish also. The vicar will, at the end of the three Sundays, give the Groom a certificate to say that the banns have been read. This certificate must be given to the vicar who is conducting the service; this can be done as late as the day before the wedding, but it is best handed over well beforehand. The marriage cannot go ahead without this certificate, for which there is a small legal fee.

There is no problem if one partner is a member of a Free Church; the vicar conducting the ceremony can arrange everything but sometimes it may be necessary to go to the Register Office. However if the Free Church partner lives outside the parish then the rule in the above paragraph still applies. If you are both members of Church of England churches but neither of you lives in the parish where you will be married, then banns must be read in all three churches! Or you may need a certificate from the Superintendent Registrar. The vicar concerned will advise you.

A marriage in Scotland

There are at least two important differences if you are getting married in Scotland. The first is that it is not the building that has to be approved for weddings, but the person who conducts the wedding service. This means that the service does not have to take place in a church; it can take place in a hotel, a home or even unlikely places like the top of a mountain!

The second difference is that a Registrar does not have to be present. Instead you have to go to the Registrar's Office and obtain what is called 'the Marriage Schedule'. When you give this to the approved person who is to conduct your wedding service, he may then marry you, providing you have the two necessary witnesses over the age of 16.

The steps to take, therefore, are as follows: first, see the person who is to conduct your marriage service, and fix the date. Then, between four to six weeks before the marriage date contact the Registrar for the district where the marriage is to take place. The Registrar will give you a 'marriage notice' for each of you to complete and submit. This marriage notice must not be returned to the Registrar later than fifteen days prior to the marriage. Once the Registrar has received that notice, and is satisfied that there is no legal impediment to the marriage, and that the person who is to solemnise the marriage is approved, he will prepare and issue a Marriage Schedule. One of you must personally attend at the Registrar's Office to receive it. It is then your responsibility to give the Marriage Schedule to the person conducting your marriage service. He cannot marry you without it. So that you do not forget to bring it on the day, you may feel happier by giving it to him a day or so before. You will have a lot of other things to think about on your wedding day!

It is your responsibility to arrange for the schedule to be returned to the issuing Registrar within three days after the marriage. You will be given an envelope with the appropriate address on it. If the person conducting your wedding does not suggest returning it for you, we would recommend that you ask a reliable friend to do so. A Best Man who returns his hired suit without removing the envelope first is not the best person! You will receive your marriage certificate from the Registrar in due course.

A marriage in Northern Ireland

In Presbyterian Churches in Northern Ireland marriages normally take place either by an ordinary Licence or a Special Licence. The ordinary Licence is valid for one month and allows for the marriage to take place within a registered Presbyterian church building and within a specified Presbytery area. The marriage may take place between 8.0am and 6.0pm. A Special Licence is valid for three months and allows for the marriage at any time and in any place or building throughout Northern Ireland.

For an ***ordinary Licence*** the Bride or Groom must have been a member of a Presbyterian congregation for at least one month before the application and one of you must have been resident for at least fifteen days within the Presbytery of the church at which you will be married. The first step is to complete a 'Notice of Marriage' with your minister and the certificate is then taken to one of the Licensing Ministers in your Presbytery; this must be done at least eight days before the wedding. The Licensing Minister will issue a Licence of Marriage which must be given to the minister who is to officiate at the wedding.

For a ***Special Licence*** at least one of you must be a member of a Presbyterian Church in Northern Ireland. There are no time or residential requirements and the minister's 'Notice of Marriage' is not needed. If you are members of The Presbyterian Church in Ireland, the forms you need to complete can be obtained from the General Secretary's Office, Church House, Belfast, BT1 6DW. You should note that if neither of you are connected with a Presbyterian Church in Northern Ireland, or if one of you is a foreign national, a Roman Catholic, or of another faith, or is divorced, there may be a delay whilst enquiries are made—so allow time.

The Methodist Church and the Church of Ireland are similar to the Presbyterian Church. The arrangement for Baptist and Independent Evangelical Churches is the same as that for England and Wales. In all cases the two witnesses at the wedding must be over 16 years of age.

Please note that the above regulations may change if, as is expected, new political arrangements come into force in Northern Ireland.

Your vows and the law

Because your marriage is a social contract in which society witnesses your promises to each other and agrees to recognise you as husband and wife, there are parts of your service that are in the form of a legal contract. In the Free Church marriage service there are two parts that are compulsory for the minister to take you through:

The first part contains **the words of declaration,** in which you both declare that you know of no reason why you should not be married. You have a choice of wording and it is wise to discuss with the officiating minister or leader your preferences, and his, beforehand. The traditional words are, 'I do solemnly declare that I know not of any lawful impediment why I (full names) may not be joined in matrimony to (full names)'. Alternatively you may say, 'I declare that I know of no legal reason why I (full names) may not be joined in marriage to (full names)'. Or you may simply respond, 'I am' in answer to the question 'Are you (full names) free lawfully to marry (full names)?' Whichever form you choose, both the Groom and Bride repeat the declaration.

The second part contains **the words of contract**, which you each repeat. They are, 'I call upon these persons here present to witness that I (full names) do take thee (full names) to be my lawful wedded wife/husband'. An alternative is, 'I (full names) take you (full names) to be my wedded wife/husband'. Or you may say, 'I (full names) take thee (full names) to be my wedded wife/husband'.

The minister may add to both these vows, both before and after, but he must include these words exactly as we have them here; without them your marriage is not legally valid.

In the Church of England there is a little difference, because here the marriage must be performed 'according to the rites of the Church of England'. There are now three possible services to choose from, but the basic pattern is the same. First the vicar will, during the three Sundays of reading the banns, ask the congregation to speak out if they know 'cause or just impediment' why the two people in question may not be married. Then, on the day of the wedding, he will repeat this and the couple will pledge to take each other as husband and wife 'Till death us do part'. Then will follow the giving of the rings and the vicar will pronounce them husband and wife in the name of the Trinity. Incidentally, whether in the Free Church or the Church of England, if anyone does object to the marriage during the service it is left entirely to the discretion of the minister whether or not to proceed. He is under no legal obligation to stop the proceedings.

Remember that in a service in any place of worship there are still certain forms of words that must, by law, be used. Your minister or vicar will, of course, know all about this and it need not trouble you. However, you should ask for a copy of the full service and vows and go through them carefully together. You will never make more important promises.

You need two witnesses to sign the register. They do not have to be over eighteen, though they should be responsible people who are able to understand that they are witnessing a marriage. To avoid any hassle with relatives who might think they should sign, it is often a good idea to invite the Best Man and the Chief Bridesmaid to act as witnesses. We have never known anyone to be offended by this; although the vicar or Authorized Person may prefer the two fathers since he already has their full names in front of him. However, the choice is yours.

The church and your wedding

Whether in a Free Church or the Church of England, the minister must always be the first person you call on. It all starts with that phone call, or the brief request as you leave church one Sunday, to have an appointment to see him. It is nice, but not essential, if you can both arrange to meet him together. When you do meet the minister to clear a date and time, he will then inform you of all details that you need to be aware of regarding weddings in that church.

For various reasons, you may want another minister to take some part in the service. Remember that you can by all means make a request, but your minister must have the final responsibility of saying yes or no. In the event of a 'division of duties' it is more normal for the visiting minister to preach the sermon, whilst the resident man conducts the actual marriage; but this is not a rigid rule. Whatever you do, don't approach the visiting man until you have spoken to your minister; this is discourteous and can be embarrassing.

There are no set ministry or church fees in many of the Free Churches, but don't forget to ask about it right at the beginning; this can avoid misunderstanding later. In the Church of England there will be some set fees, and there are extras for things like the choir and the bells. Be sure to ask about all this right from the start.

You will probably want to choose your own hymns, but again, don't forget that the courteous thing is to check these, and the order of service, with the minister before you get an order printed. Similarly it may be a good idea to have some item during the signing of the register. Whether or not the register is signed in the church as part of the service (an increasingly common practice today), or in the vestry towards the close of the service, it is a good idea to consider an appropriate singing item, or even some Scripture or other verses read. Alternatively you may simply draw attention to the items that the organist will play. Don't forget to book the pianist or organist as soon as you have cleared a date with the minister. If you want to use a friend as the musician, it is courteous to explain this to the 'resident' organist right at the start.

Jobs for all

There are certain long-established customs and traditions associated with weddings. Some of them are nothing more than tradition and you may or may not dispense with these. Others are superstition, and a Christian couple will not want to include these. But some are sound common sense or simple courtesy, and you will be well advised to think carefully before you trample over people's feelings or expectations.

We have set out for you here some of the duties that traditionally fall to the people involved in your wedding. Of course there will always be room for changes, and we will indicate some of these as we go along.

The Bride and Groom

You will want to do as much as possible together. It is unfair of a Groom to leave everything to his Bride (or vice versa) and this may be a bad sign for the future! First of all you must together approach the minister concerning the marriage service and choose your organist, hymns and music. You are both responsible for making sure the marriage is duly registered in the way we have described under 'Your Marriage and the Law'. Although the Bride's parents are responsible for sending out the invitations, you may want to do this yourselves just for the fun of it. You may also want to arrange for the invitations and order of service sheets to be printed. In any case, together you must help draw up a wedding guest list and a gift list. We will come back to these points later.

The Groom

The Bridegroom is responsible for choosing his Best Man and the Ushers. The Best Man may be a brother, close relative, or just a good friend. You should never feel 'obliged' to ask a particular person. Have the Best Man you would really like, not the one that is expected of you. Perhaps you will need to have a quiet word with, let's say, a brother who may be 'miffed' that you didn't ask him; simply explain your close and long friendship with Bill and how you would like him because of this. Remember that a Best Man does have important duties and therefore it is not just enough that he is a good friend. Can he take command and is he organized? If you have to organize him all the time then he will not be much help to you. If you really do want a brother or friend who is not able to undertake the duties of a Best Man, why not appoint a Master of Ceremonies to run your reception; this is done in some parts of Scotland where the minister acts as MC.

The Groom also buys the rings and pays all the fees and other expenses except for the church flowers. He pays for the bouquets for the Bride and her Bridesmaids and also a little 'thank-you' present for the Bridesmaids, Best Man and other friends; he may like to buy the Ushers matching ties as a gift for the occasion. The Groom is responsible for arranging transport for the Bride and her father, the Bridesmaids, and himself and the Best Man. It is a courtesy also for him to make sure that the Bride's mother has someone to take her to church; it is a very emotional day for her, so a little spoiling is in order. If there is room, she can travel with the bridesmaids if she would like to.

It is also the Groom's responsibility to arrange for the details of the honeymoon, and check that passports are in order. There is some advice on passports in the next chapter under 'Planning your honeymoon'. The groom must also ensure that all necessary foreign currency or travellers cheques have been obtained. He ought also to have arranged for bank accounts to be held in his Bride's married name and, although we don't want to spoil your pleasurable preparations, don't forget to inform the Inland Revenue of your new status; they will catch up with you eventually, but it can save a lot of hassle if you take the initiative!

The Bride

Traditionally the Bride comes off lightly! She chooses her Bridesmaids and any Pageboys, decides on the floral decoration for the church and reception and she chooses the bouquets. Of course the Bride also arranges for her own dress and those of the Bridesmaids and Pageboys. Just a word on the Bride's dress, and those of her Bridesmaids—they should be modest. There is nothing better than a Bride you can look at and admire, without thinking that you should not be looking at her!

Again, we encourage you to choose the Bridesmaids you will be happy with, and turn a deaf ear to all the hints and innuendoes about who you ought to have. It is your day and don't let anyone spoil it for you. It may seem nice to have lots of little Bridesmaids, but don't forget that they may be more of a hindrance than a help, and if they are very small you may have them running all over the place. In any case, make sure that you have a chief Bridesmaid who will be calm and helpful to you on the day; you will greatly value this.

The Bride's parents

A heavy burden falls upon the Bride's parents. They are responsible for arranging and paying for the reception. This is a very expensive item in these days whatever kind of reception you have. Because of this, it is quite common for the Groom's parents to approach the Bride's parents and offer to share in the cost of the reception; if the young couple want something special then they must be prepared to help as well. So much depends upon the financial resources of the parents; and remember, the two sets of parents may be in a very different financial position. Be sensitive to this and don't expect too much, unless you are prepared to pay for it. If the Groom's parents are willing to help with the reception costs then the Groom's father should make the approach; the approach cannot come from the Bride's father.

If the Groom's parents are willing to help with the reception costs then the Groom's father should make the approach

Make sure everyone understands this from the start. Be specific; it is no use offering vaguely to 'help towards the costs'. What, in pounds and pence does that mean? It will save a lot of embarrassment and ill-feeling later on if everybody knows where they stand. We suggest you write a memo of what has been agreed and let everyone involved have a copy. It is also a nice courtesy for the Bride's parents to keep in regular contact with the Groom's parents so that they know what is happening. It is good for them to be consulted from time to time and made to feel part of everything. Weddings are notorious affairs for rows and angry scenes, especially as everyone gets keyed-up as the day approaches. The Bride's parents can do so much to make everyone feel 'in touch' and wanted. There is nothing worse than the Groom's parents not knowing what is happening and not feeling free to ask.

The Groom's parents

There are no specific duties for the Groom's parents, although as we have already indicated, it is increasingly common today for them to offer to help share the cost of the wedding. If the two sets of parents do not know each other well, it is an excellent idea for them all to spend an evening together, with the Bride and Groom. This should merely be an informal and relaxed evening where everyone gets to know everyone, it should not be the occasion for detailed planning.

It is a long-standing custom that the Bride is 'given away' by her father during the marriage ceremony. This goes back to the days when the young woman was considered to be under the care and protection of her father until her marriage. Today many girls have left home long before their wedding day. There is no necessity for this part of the service; however, the Bride can hardly walk down the aisle on her own. Some couples prefer to meet at the back of the church and walk down the aisle together. On the other hand the old custom still has a lot of merit in a Christian wedding. It provides a clear picture of family bonds when the Bride comes in with her father, and an equally plain statement of the new relationship when she is 'given away' to her husband. We recommend its value, and most fathers' appreciate their privilege. Where there is no father who can undertake this task, a senior relative or family friend can take on the role. In this case it must be the Bride's choice.

The Best Man

The Best Man is a key figure at the wedding since he is the right-hand man for the Groom. Throughout the preparations he should keep closely in touch with the Groom and should spend some time with him to make sure that he is aware of all the instructions the Groom may wish to give him. On the wedding day he should call for the Groom in good time and make sure that they do not arrive at the church later than twenty minutes prior to the service.

It is important that the Best Man carries out his duties efficiently. He will stand beside the Groom during the service and must have the rings ready to offer to the minister at the appropriate time. At the close of the service he must see the Bride and Groom safely away to the reception and then make sure that the Bridesmaids are shown to their car. Similarly he should take care that the parents leave the church easily and that all the guests have transport. He is responsible for paying any fees that are required on the day; these should be carefully labelled in sealed envelopes. He is also responsible for the Ushers to whom he can delegate many of these duties.

At the reception the Best Man should ensure that the guests meet the Bride and Groom, but it is wise for him to remain close to the couple so that if a guest is taking too much time over this he can politely move the offender forward! Unless your reception is a formal affair with a master of ceremonies and a toastmaster, the Best Man is responsible for calling the guests to attention as the Bride and Groom enter, for giving any general notices necessary regarding the form of serving at the reception, and for saying grace or calling on the man who will. The Best Man will also inform the guests that the cake is about to be cut, and will be responsible for reading any greetings or cards that need to be read (generally only from absent friends) and introducing the speeches. We will have more to say about the reception in the next chapter.

The Best Man announces when the couple are ready to leave the reception and also informs the guests when they have returned from changing and are ready to leave for their honeymoon, though many guests will have already departed to the car park! When the couple have finally left, the Best Man should thank the caterers, pay any gratuities appropriate, and make sure that the parents are taken care of, not forgetting to thank the Bride's parents for the reception. He should not leave the reception until all the guests have left.

From all this it will be obvious that a good Best Man will be quietly efficient, patient and courteous, and yet able to command attention and be heard at the reception. He should be thoughtful and ever watching for something that has been overlooked or someone who is feeling out of place or awkward. The Groom should never find himself giving instructions on the wedding day, if he wants something done, he whispers his request to the Best Man who immediately acts on his behalf.

A good Best Man will be quietly efficient, patient and courteous, and yet able to command attention and be heard at the reception

The Best Man is well advised to write down the various things he must do during the day and constantly refer to his list. His is a very important role and he should not take it lightly.

The Ushers (sometimes called Stewards)

Once the Groom has chosen his Ushers he should begin to write out a list of duties for them. They should be at the church not later than forty-five minutes prior to the service and they may need to keep the front of the church clear for official cars. Some local police stations are willing to lend official cones to help with this, but you must make sure they are returned immediately after use or you will find the facility quickly withdrawn.

In some churches, a caretaker or his equivalent will do all that is necessary in preparing the church for a wedding; this may include keeping the front of the church free of parked cars early in the morning. However, in many Free Churches the Ushers may have to take responsibility for preparing the church and changing the seating arrangements. Ask the minister for instructions and don't forget to enquire about the best time to make these preparations the evening before. The church may be in use early in the evening, and your Ushers must be willing to wait until a convenient time. Remember that any alterations to seating etc. must be put back before the next day. It is also a courtesy to the caretaker or cleaner to offer to sweep up any confetti and to leave the church neat and tidy. A church can actually be fined for causing litter if too much confetti is left on the pavement, so it is wise to enquire whether the church has a policy on this. The same may be true of a reception car park or forecourt.

The duties of the Ushers on the day may include one outside to direct cars and open doors for passengers; one inside the church entrance lobby to give 'buttonholes' to guests (if you are providing these), and two in the church itself to give each member of the congregation an order of service and to show them to a seat. It is customary for Ushers to enquire discreetly: 'Are you friends of the Bride or Groom?' Bride's friends and relatives sit on the left of the church, and the Groom's on the right. If guests declare that they are friends of both, then the Ushers should use their discretion in trying to fill the church evenly on both sides.

It is most important that the Chief Usher should show the Groom's parents to their seats when they arrive, and the Bride's mother to her seat; she will be the last guest to arrive, just before the Bride. The seating of the Bride's mother is normally the sign that the Bride and her father are ready to enter the church.

The Ushers should remain on duty throughout the service, directing late-comers to a seat at a convenient point in the service, and afterwards they should ensure that all guests who have been invited to the reception leave the church and know exactly where they are going. It is always a great help for a printed map, clearly marked and accurate, to be available to guests after the service if they are not familiar with the locality. Incidentally it is a great help if these directions, and directions to locate the church and nearest car park, are sent out with the invitations.

Ushers should be dressed smartly, and as we have indicated, the Groom may consider buying them matching ties. It is always a good idea to appoint one of them as the Chief Usher and then the Best Man knows who he can liaise with if he needs to give any last minute instructions. The Ushers should also take charge of any presents that arrive at the time of the service and ensure that they are taken to whichever home the Groom requests. Cards and other messages of greeting that arrive at the service should be handed to the Best Man who will consult with the Groom as to whether or not they are to be read out.

The Ushers should also be on duty at the reception to assist guests in finding their seats.

The Bridesmaids

The Bridesmaids are not intended only to look pretty and add colour to the occasion, though they will certainly do this. The Chief Bridesmaid will not only help the Bride dress on the morning, but she will be constantly attending to the Bride throughout the day. During the service she takes the Bride's bouquet and then gives it back to her at the appropriate time. She will make sure the Bride's train and veil are spread out correctly, and if the Bride wears a veil over her face, it is her duty to lift it back after they are announced as husband and wife, unless the Groom prefers to do this. Throughout the day she will be watching the Bride and will not hesitate to attend discreetly to anything out of place.

Other Bridesmaids will be responsible for the Bride's train also and any further duties that the Bride requests of them.

Your photographer

Finding a photographer in whom you know you will have full confidence is a hard task, and sorting out who is most competitive in price is almost impossible. This is not because there are few good photographers, on the contrary, it is because there are so many, and their price structures are so different. Some photographers charge for their time and the prints you choose, some give their time free but will therefore charge more for the prints; others will offer an album of, say, thirty pictures for a set price, and still others will include an engagement picture as well. It is all very puzzling!

The best approach is to decide approximately how many prints you will want in your album, not less than two dozen we suggest, and then compare how much they would all charge for this finished product. Alternatively you may set your budget and then ask them what you will get for it.

Start by talking with a few friends who have recently got married and learn from their experience. Look through their albums and decide if you like the kind of photography you see there. Then visit a few local studios and talk with the actual photographer. This is important. It is not good enough to be told that 'one of the team' will be on duty for your wedding. You want to know which one and then meet him or her. Can you relax with him or her? Or are they domineering? A photographer can spoil your day by getting all the guests angry with an over-bossy approach.

Be warned! Don't leave it too long before booking a photographer. After clearing the date with your minister and booking your reception, the photographer must be next on your list. A good photographer can be booked up eighteen months ahead. Don't leave it to a friend or relative whose hobby is photography. You may save some money, but lose a record of a wonderful day! A professional photographer's charges may seem a lot, but they are trained to avoid mistakes.

When you visit the photographer, tell him that nearer the time you will provide a list of pictures you would especially like. A good photographer will be glad of this. At a mutually agreed time (he won't expect it twelve months beforehand!), present a neatly typed copy and go through it so that it is fully understood. Keep a copy for yourselves. Once again, a good photographer will visit your reception venue beforehand, if it is not already familiar to him.

Here is a sample of what your list might include, but of course this is only a guide; you will want to personalise it:

Pictures at the Bride's home.

★ Two portraits of the Bride.
★ Detail of the Bride's dress and bouquet (often overlooked by photographers).
★ Chief Bridesmaid, or Bride's mother, helping Bride with the veil.
★ Leaving home with father.

Pictures at church

★ Groom and Best Man arriving.
★ Groom, Best Man and Ushers.
★ Some guests arriving.
★ Parents arriving.
★ Bridesmaids arriving.
★ Bride and father arriving.
★ Exchanging rings.
★ Signing register.
★ Bride, Groom and minister.
★ Bride and Groom coming down the aisle.
For these last four items be sure to ask the minister if he has no objection to photographs in the church. Please abide by his decision.
★ Outside the church or at the reception.
★ Bride and Groom.
★ Bridal party (Bride, Groom, Best Man, Bridesmaids, Pageboys).
★ Bridal party with parents (there is no end to the mix here i.e. Bride with her parents, Groom with his etc.)
★ Other groups of friends and relatives.
★ Leaving the church by car.

Pictures at the reception

★ The cake (both general and a close-up of detail).
★ Cutting the cake (nearly always taken before the guests arrive).
★ Guests entering and greeted by the Bride and Groom.
★ Head table.
★ Particular guest-groups (an usher should be delegated to help the photographer identify the groups or tables you especially want photographed).
★ Bride and Groom leaving the reception for their honeymoon. (Your photographer will normally have left long before this. If you expect the photographer to stay throughout the reception, or at least to the first part of it, to take group pictures, make this clear from the start; and be prepared to pay considerably more for his extra time. It could be worth another wedding to him).

Make a particular point of asking for a close-up of the Bride's dress, including a back view. The careful lace-work or pattern on some dresses are often overlooked; and on a bright day in full sunlight it can be difficult to capture. The best time would be in the Bride's home before she leaves. Similarly a close-up of the detail of the Bride's bouquet and the cake will be treasured pictures.

This list is only a guide and you must make it your own. But you can see how easily you use up thirty or more prints.

There was a custom some years ago for the photographer to come back to the reception with the proofs. It may have been good for business, but it was bad for the reception; besides, coming home to see the album is something to look forward to on your honeymoon. Incidentally, please give the photographer clear instructions as to who, if anyone, will be collecting the proofs while you are away. Photographers are embarrassed by relatives demanding the pictures. Clear instructions saves problems.

Videos and recordings

This is the video age, and you may want to hire a professional video recordist, or even let a friend take a video for you. However, never let a video take the place of the photographer; you will always want those still pictures. Remember also that a video camera is not like a still camera, and it can prove a great distraction and intrusion. Check that your minister has no objection to the use of video in the church, and also check with the cameraman that he doesn't require special lighting. At the reception never allow the camera to run continuously. Guests will find it off-putting and even embarrassing. Allow the cameraman a fixed time to get his film and disappear!

If you do decide to have a video made, as a matter of courtesy inform your official photographer of this.

We strongly advise you to have your service recorded. You will certainly regret it if you don't. Make sure that the microphone is close by those taking part so that all the responses are clearly heard. A separate microphone for congregational singing is a decided advantage! Most churches will have their own recording equipment so make sure you ask about this and don't just assume that your service will be recorded.

Printing, recordings, and the law

There is a very important matter of the **copyright laws** relating to your printing, video or audio recording. If you have a printed order of service and use modern hymns or songs you will require copyright permission. Many churches hold a licence from the Christian Copyright Licensing at 26 Gildredge Road, Eastbourne, East Sussex, BN21 4SA (01323-417711. e-mail info@ccli.co.uk.). This licence allows the church to use many of the modern songs and hymns.

However, the licence does not cover the use of recordings of services, whether on video or sound. According to the law, if you wish to use music that is copyright, or record a service which will include words or music for which someone currently holds the copyright, you will require a licence from the Mechanical Copyright Protection Society Ltd. at Elgar House, 41 Streatham High Road, London SW16 1ER (0181-769-4400). Unless the church already holds a licence from the MCPS—which is unlikely—you will need to write to them giving the name of the church and the date of your wedding and requesting a Private Function Licence. A small fee is charged and you should phone to ask the current rate as no licence will be issued unless you send a cheque. This Private Function Licence will give you permission to use and record any words and music, they do not need to know what pieces you will use. You will be allowed to make up to twenty-five video or audio copies. This will also cover any live music at your reception. Just to complicate matters, this licence does not cover you to record recorded music! Remember that no copyright licence is required after seventy-five years from the death of an author or composer. So if yours is a traditional wedding, you should be safe!

This is only a brief summary of the important laws relating to copyright and you are advised to write to the addresses given above to clarify the position in your particular case.

Planning your reception

What kind of reception?

The types and styles of wedding receptions are so varied that it would be impossible for us to detail them here. They range from a small home-made buffet for a dozen relatives and close friends, to a large formal dinner for a hundred and fifty or more guests. It all depends on your preference and your budget. Nothing is customary, you make your own choice. Rigid formalities are beginning to break down. For example the seating at the Bride and Groom's table is traditionally that of the Bride's father sitting with the Groom's mother to signify the joining of two families; however sometimes the Bride's parents sit together with the Groom and vice versa.

There are some things to bear in mind when planning the kind of reception you want.

The informal buffet where guests are free to move around and talk as they wish has many advantages. You will generally find people stay in their small groups, therefore you need to be alert to those who are on their own and who may find the reception a great strain. The formal lunch can overcome this problem, providing you are sensitive in the allocation of places.

It can be very attractive to decide on a do-it-yourself buffet style reception in the church hall. This is certainly the cheapest kind of reception although you need to be careful. If there is a charge for the use of the hall, and if all the crockery, cutlery and glasses etc. have to be hired, you can find that the price in the end will not greatly differ from a modest professional reception. The idea of planning it all and doing it all yourselves may have its appeal, but be warned that there is far more work involved than you ever expected. We suggest you talk with those who have already self-catered before you make your final decision. Only very careful planning can avoid your good idea becoming a tragedy of misunderstandings and last minute hassle. You need someone in charge who is the essence of tact, patience, and organizational ability. We are not trying to put you off, but you must be realistic.

If you decide to go in the DIY direction, make sure you have a good leader with an excellent team. Preferably do not let one of the mothers be in charge, as the workload and responsibility can spoil the wedding for them. But some mothers thrive on all this and who are we to stop them! However, we want to emphasise that it places a lot of strain on the Bride's mother, and a number of mothers have commented to us that they would never have taken it on had they been aware of the headache it would prove to be. So much has to be left to the last minute because you only have the hall for one day, and possibly late the previous evening. If you hire the hall for two days to make life easier for you, you will be closing the financial gap between DIY and a catering firm to take the headache away from you. Work it out carefully.

If you decide to hire a hall plus outside caterers, you will probably find it only a little more expensive to use a hotel or restaurant where they will do everything for you. Talk with friends who have recently got married, make lots of phone calls to check out prices, and then visit, by appointment, those that you consider most within your range. Talk with the catering manager about your needs and you will soon decide whether you feel relaxed and comfortable with their approach. If you plan to have no alcohol at your reception then make this clear right from the start; you may notice their enthusiasm wane immediately, if so, avoid that venue! On the other hand, if they take your request for no alcohol in a matter-of-fact and understanding way then you will probably get on well with them. But remember that most caterers hope to make a large profit on the sale of drinks, so you must expect them to put a heavy surcharge on soft drinks and fruit juice. Find out their costs at this first meeting.

Having decided upon your venue and caterers, get everything in writing and be clear as to when you pay a deposit, how much, when they require final numbers, whether you are free to provide your own floral decorations for the tables, when can you bring the cake to them and so on. It is important to put everything in writing because you may be booking a year or more ahead, and memories fail long before then. Incidentally, if you are getting married at a popular time of the year (Easter and Summer) you may encounter difficulty in finding someone to cater for you, so don't waste time before you choose a venue. Put this high on your list of priorities.

As the Guests arrive

At your reception the Bride and Groom should always be the first to arrive, ready to greet the guests. Also, the photographer will want to take pictures before the guests come in. It is customary for the parents, Best Man and Bridesmaids to be there as well when the guests arrive. However a formal line-up can be time-consuming and tedious for guests. This is another formality that some couples prefer to break with. Whatever you decide, let your caterers know your plan because they may be allowing at least an hour for these introductions. If you do have this line-up please make sure your guests are not queuing outside in the cold; you must have an informal gathering area for them. A traditional 'line-up' would be: the Bride's father with the Groom's mother and next to them the Groom's father with the Bride's mother. Then comes the Bride and Groom, with the Best Man, as ever, close by. The Bridesmaids can stand discreetly apart; not all the guests will need to meet them. A less formal alternative is for the Bride and Groom to be the first to be met, with the parents a short distance away either separately or together, and the Bridesmaids, again, discreetly apart. The Best Man may be employed ensuring that people keep moving.

Speeches ... and more Speeches

Sadly we have to comment that many receptions can become an embarrassing bore. There are a number of reasons for this. First of all, they often go on far too long. If you seat your guests opposite total strangers with whom they have nothing in common, and they are expected to make polite conversation for three or four hours, even the most talkative can begin to run dry. If a guest is on his own and everyone is talking around him, the whole thing can become a personal disaster. In addition to this, speeches are sometimes long, boring, irrelevant, and the attempted jokes embarrassingly unfunny.

Receptions can follow the same monotonous pattern of most other receptions.

Don't relate embarrassing personal details of the Bride or Groom, it can be very insensitive and is rarely funny

So, a few warnings:

Don't allow all kinds of people to give speeches by inviting any guest to stand up and talk. They will—at length.

Don't try to be funny or tell jokes—unless you are a 'natural'.

Don't relate embarrassing personal details of the Bride or Groom, it can be very insensitive and is rarely funny.

Don't ask anyone to give a speech unless they can give it well and briefly. Four minutes is quite long enough for any speech at the reception. Tell everyone how long they have got! Speeches should be sincere. Those who are Christians will probably want to bring in a reference to the Lord's care and love, but this is not the time for a long sermon or an obvious dig at the unbelievers present. Courtesy, sincerity, brevity and joy will be long remembered by the guests.

Who gives a speech?

The Bride's Father, who generally has provided the reception, thanks everyone for coming and makes a few pleasant remarks about his daughter and his new son-in-law.

The Groom thanks the Bride's parents for his wife and for the reception. He can acknowledge his debt to his own parents. He should thank the guests for their presents, cards and warm expressions of love. He also thanks the

Bridesmaids for being such a help to his wife and compliments them on their attractiveness.

The Best Man may express his pleasure at being asked to help the Groom on this special day. He should respond on behalf of the Bridesmaids and then read out any greetings or important cards from a few absent friends. There is no need to read greetings from those who are at the reception; and if there are absent friends or relatives who sent greetings, the Best Man must make it his business to know what the relationship is. He should not make fun of the absent 'Great Aunt Matilda'.

Why not make your reception a little different? If the minister is present, don't ask him to say grace; a greater impression is made by another friend or relative taking this part. Why not do away entirely with the traditional toasts? They are totally meaningless and pagan in origin. As an alternative the Best Man could explain that as Christians we have a more positive way of expressing our hopes for the couple, and that is by prayer. He may then lead the guests in prayer or call upon a close friend to do so. As with grace before the meal, don't ask the minister to do this, he has already prayed for the couple in church and it is more significant for someone else to pray now.

We advise against following your reception with an informal late-night buffet for your friends. We know this is becoming increasingly popular, but it makes the day far too long for the Bride and Groom. A late night party can be a disaster for your first night together. Plan to be at your destination early enough to enjoy a leisurely evening together. Your first night as husband and wife should not be spoilt by being hurried, late and exhausted. You can plan a special 'reception' for the wider group of friends after your honeymoon.

Alcohol and your Reception

Christian weddings are increasingly using alcohol at the reception but why not be different and ban it? This will:

Avoid Uncle Harry showing himself up as he usually does.

Avoid embarrassment or offence to any of your Christian friends who are teetotal.

Avoid the possibility of starting a young Christian on the alcohol road.

Give you the fun of discovering alternative and attractive drinks.

Some may joke about the absence of alcohol but the majority of guests will not mind, and those who stay away because of this you are better without.

If you must have alcohol because parents insist on it, or you want it, make sure that your friends know there are alternative drinks provided. Give very clear instructions to the caterers to ask guests whether they would prefer a non-alcoholic drink. Both must be served together. It is insulting to be met at the reception by a waitress offering a glass of sherry, and if you request a fruit juice to be told, 'It's over there'. Any tray should contain both drinks. Non-alcohol drinkers are not second-class guests. If you do have toasts, they do not have to be drunk in champagne; apple juice or water is just as polite. Remember, some of your guests will not readily distinguish an alcoholic drink from a non-alcoholic one, so caterers must be told to make it clear what they are serving. We have seen Christians embarrassed and offended by mistakenly sipping the wrong drink. We have also experienced a breach of courtesy on the part of a caterer who insisted that you can't drink a toast with water—he soon learnt that you can!

Seating

Whilst long formal tables are common, the circular table, seating ten or a dozen guests, is probably the best seating arrangement. These tables give guests the maximum opportunity of talking with the maximum number of people, but a shy guest who wants to sit quietly will not feel too embarrassed because they will not be staring at someone directly opposite. Normally *someone* can keep conversation going on a table of ten!

This brings you to the problem of yet another list: ***The Seating List.*** You will need to present this to the caterers at least the day before the wedding together with the named place-cards. Be warned: it is not a five minute job! It is not even a two hour job. In preparing this list your primary objective is to give all your guests the happiest reception possible. With this in mind place people together who either know each other or who have something in common. Remember, at a long table you can only easily talk with one or two people opposite and one on either side of you. If you are at the end of the table your choice is even more limited. Don't sit Christian friends opposite non-Christian friends and relatives so that they can 'witness'. Receptions are not easy places for this. Your whole service and reception should be a witness to God's goodness and his gospel. On the other hand don't segregate. A sensitive and thoughtful mix is best. It is not very clever to place the minister opposite the most aggressive atheist in the family!

Place people together who either know each other or who have something in common

Caring for your Guests

Allow yourselves time to leave the head table and chat with your guests. This is especially essential if you dispensed with the formal line-up as guests came in. There is a golden rule here: *Hold hands and stay together.* Guests will want to talk with you both, and friends or relatives unknown to one partner can be introduced by the other. If you *hold hands all the time* then you can never be separated. How often we have heard the plaintive cry of a harassed Bride: 'Where is Peter now?' Peter is busy chatting to his cronies at another table. Keep together; hold hands; and don't stay at one table for too long. Try to get round all the guests in groups, however briefly. Maybe a wise Best Man can keep his eye on this and gently move the couple on if they are spending too long in one place. It is best to have this 'walk-about' before you go to change. People want to see the Bride's dress for as long as possible and, anyway, it is a good conversation piece.

Time your reception carefully. Be sensitive to guests who have a long way to travel; it can be helpful to let guests know in advance what time the reception is scheduled to end.

Never keep guests waiting whilst you travel half an hour to change. Arrange a room at the reception or somewhere locally. Go together. Remember, the young husband has not yet been alone with his new wife and he has not had time to admire her dress; besides, he longs to give her a cuddle and a kiss. It will also help to overcome possible embarrassment later if he has helped her out of her wedding dress. But don't be too long; your guests are still waiting to see you off. Traditionally they should not leave the reception until you have departed for your honeymoon.

If you have a really able Christian soloist, group, or instrumentalist, why not use them at the reception? This can be a very pleasant interlude and it will help everyone to relax. But it must be first class.

Wedding flowers

A florist needs to be booked between three and six months prior to your wedding date; and even more if you have chosen a popular time of the year. If you want to be sure that everything will match in colour, you would be well advised to use the same florist for all your flowers: bouquets, church and reception. If possible let your florist have a piece of the bridesmaids dress material; if you are buying dresses, buy also a length of matching ribbon to give to the florist and to anyone else who may be helping with the flowers. It is also a wise course to check with the person responsible what is and is not allowed in the church, and where flowers can and cannot be placed. Make sure that arrangements have been made for your florist to have access to the church the day prior to the wedding and also access to any equipment you have arranged to borrow, for example the church flower pedestal.

Flowers at the reception vary according to the size and decor of the hall, the number of tables, and your available budget. As a guide you will require one arrangement on each circular table, and two or three on a long table. If you have booked caterers, they often have their own florist, so discuss this with them and let them know whether you are making your own arrangements for the flowers. If you are having a buffet reception, you will need one or two arrangements for each buffet table. You will also require arrangements for the head table; though remember that the bouquets of the Bride and Bridesmaids will be placed on the head table, so there is space for you to cut back on expense here if you wish.

Any room can be made attractive with flowers, whatever the time of year; but flowers are very expensive so be sure to discuss your budget carefully with the florist so that you do not get an unpleasant shock when the bill arrives.

High quality silk flowers are an excellent option with many advantages. Bouquets and table arrangements can be made well in advance. They can also be kept for many years as a memento of your special day. If you want fresh flowers, remember that they have to be delivered and arranged within twenty-four hours of your wedding day so you may be advised to avoid Mothers' Day and Easter when flowers are very expensive.

High quality silk flowers are an excellent option with many advantages.

If you have someone among your family or friends whose hobby is flower arranging, why not ask them to help. They would enjoy doing it. But discuss with them what you want and what you can afford so that there will be no misunderstanding later. They may spend many hours on arranging your flowers and could well give you a better display than a florist has time for. A monetary gift or gift-token would always be appreciated.

You may decide to make some of your arrangements available as thank-you gifts, or as gifts for the two mothers and other special relatives or friends. A lovely, never-forgotten, touch is made when two Bridesmaids present the two mothers with bouquets during the reception; but to help with your finances these can be the two specially made arrangements from the head table. Arrange all this beforehand and give a list to someone who will take charge of it for you.

There is a lot of work and skill employed in making bouquets, so if you want to be sure that they will look good and stay in one piece throughout the day, we strongly advise you to use a qualified florist for these. She will give you a book of shapes and designs to choose from, and often photographs of previous wedding bouquets that she has made. Be guided by the florist. If you are small, a large bouquet will swamp you, and if you are very tall then a small bouquet can look ridiculous. Sometimes the Bride will give her bouquet to her mother or grandmother. This is far better than the tradition of throwing the bouquet! If the bouquet is composed of fresh flowers it can be dried or the flowers pressed to make a picture; but this has to be done immediately and is very expensive.

Many Brides and Bridesmaids overlook the correct way to hold their bouquet. Your arms should drop naturally so that the top of the bouquet is below your waistline; it should not be clutched to your waist. If your Bridesmaids are all about the same height, practice holding the bouquets in the same position.

You may also want buttonholes for the Groom, Best Man, Ushers and the two fathers, and any other close relatives. A buttonhole for every wedding guest is an expensive luxury of the past. A nice corsage for each mother is appreciated but do make sure that the colours match the outfit! Here again, silk flowers have a great advantage. If you are privileged to have grandmothers with you, they too would greatly appreciate a nice corsage. Remember it is a very special day for them also and a little spoiling is good for them.

The wedding cake

If you are using professional caterers, discuss the wedding cake with them. They will sometimes include it in their price, so make sure you are clear about this. If you are ordering the cake as a separate item you may need to give from three to six months notice. On the other hand, a friend or relative may offer to make the cake for you. There is one important factor that should never be overlooked: if you are having more than one tier then make sure the icing is sufficiently hard to take the weight of the top tiers! You will not find it very amusing if the cake collapses a few hours prior to the reception. We have even known professionally made cakes to collapse; but there is no excuse for this. If you are in any doubt, assemble the cake for an hour or two and if the pillars have begun to mark the icing then it is too soft. In this case thin cake boards or wooden skewers will be needed to take the weight.

There are many good cake-decorating books, and you can have hours of fun choosing a design for your cake. Be careful not to overcrowd it with decorations. Some of the most attractive designs are the most simple.

It is customary to send a small slice of cake to guests who were unable to attend the wedding but who sent you a present. It is a nice little 'thank-you' gesture. You can buy small boxes for this. In any case the slices should be sent off no later than a few weeks after your wedding.

Lists... and more lists!

There are two important lists that you need to give attention to: The guest list, which contains the names of those who will be invited to the reception as guests, and the gift list which guests will ask for to guide them in choosing a wedding present for you.

The guest list

You will begin by discussing with the Bride's parents, or whoever else is taking responsibility for the reception, what kind of reception you would like (or can afford), and how many guests you would like (or can afford). Once you have fixed this number the easy part is over. How do you decide, from all your friends and relatives who to invite to attend your wedding reception, and who to leave out?

In our view the easiest and fairest way of resolving this, regardless of who is paying for the reception, is to divide the number by four. Allow an equal number of guests for the Bride to choose, the Groom to choose, and each set of parents to choose. Of course this means that the Bride and Groom have the largest number between them, but why not? It is their special day and they want to be surrounded by their friends and not merely by a host of distant and never-to-be-seen-again relatives and ancient friends of the parents. Of course there will be an overlap, since the couple will want some of the people their parents will want. If the numbers are divided equally, there should be no squabbling and jealousy between the families; and the Bride and Groom need not squabble either because they can each make their own choice, though again there will be many common friends.

Allow an equal number of guests for the Bride to choose, the Groom to choose, and each set of parents to choose

Your invitations are traditionally sent out eight weeks before the wedding, but in these days of busy diaries you may want to make it more. This is quite in order. A good stationer will provide you with a catalogue of wedding invitation styles and you can often take a catalogue home for an evening and browse through it together. Don't forget to ask how long printing takes. The catalogue will also offer you samples of wording to choose from. You can also buy matching reply cards which may encourage your guests to reply more quickly! Some guests will keep you waiting for a long time, and some will never get round to replying, although it is extremely discourteous not to reply. Don't be afraid to ring up two weeks before the date and enquire; after all, you must know your exact numbers for the caterers. Keep a few names on a reserve list so that as people decline the invitation you can send to a few more. Your skill in desk-top publishing may provide you with an economical way of designing your own invitations.

The gift list

At first you may be embarrassed at the idea of drawing up a list of presents that you want people to buy you! But for everybody's sake you must do it. After all, you don't want six cruet sets and three dozen tea-towels do you? And your guests would far rather buy you things they know you want and that they know no one else will be buying.

This list is generally the responsibility of the Bride since most of the gifts turn out to be household items. We know young Grooms complain that you never see trolley-jacks and socket sets on the gift list, but that's the way it is. However, there is no reason why these items should not be on your list. You can have hours of fun together planning your home and deciding on matching sets of this and that. Make sure the list is specific. Don't just say 'Sheets'; what colour, size, type? Tell people where they can purchase just what you want and what the current price is. Provide a good spread of prices. Include the simple and cheap items costing a few pounds, and don't be afraid to let your prices run a little beyond what you think your guests will afford. You will be surprised how generous some of your friends are. However, don't produce an extravagant and ostentatious list.

But how do you circulate the list? There are a number of possible ways and we will suggest just three:

First. It is increasingly common to make use of the helpful schemes run by many of the large departmental stores. You simply go to the store and make your gift list from their stock; you can spend hours browsing around together. Once you have your list typed out (some stores will do it for you and provide a neat folder), with careful details of type, size, colour, price etc., you present this to the assistant. You can then send copies of this to all who ask for your gift list. They simply make their selection, send their cheque to the store who then wraps and delivers the gift to your home; the store will also make sure that you do not receive duplicate gifts. All very simple. Go to your local departmental store and ask if they operate such a scheme.

Secondly. If you think this is too impersonal then you must be prepared for a little more hard work. Make your list of items and clearly indicate where they can be purchased. Now take a small exercise book with a spiral binding and cut each page horizontally across the middle. Number both halves of each page with the same number, and work through the book beginning with number 1. On each page put the details of one item that you would like, and write in the same details on the top and the bottom half. Even a picture of the item, cut from an old catalogue, can be a great help. You then simply ask people to tear out the bottom half of the page for their own information and cross out the top half. At a glance you can see what items are still left on your list. Of course you can simplify this by using one page for an item and asking them to make their choice and cross it out but not remove it. They will then have to copy out their own details.

Thirdly. The above suggestion is fine if most of your guests live locally and you can pass the list from person to person (by the way always keep in touch with it or the list will just disappear!), but what if many of the guests live a long way apart? We suggest in this case you draw up your list on a sheet of paper and have it copied. Send a copy of the master list to anyone who requests it, and ask them to phone someone you have nominated to hold the master list once they have made their choice but before they go out and buy the item. Please make sure the person in charge of the master list is readily available at the other end of the phone, or at least give the times when they will be. You can, of course, use a combination of all these suggestions.

Whilst invited guests who are unable to attend are not expected to buy a gift, many will want to do so. Also be sensitive to those who cannot afford to buy any gift at all. However, if you make sure there are plenty of low-priced items everyone should be catered for. You can make up matching sets of items by letting people know they can buy just one or two of a set. In which case you may repeat 'Three cups and saucers' of a particular set in order to get six of each. If you receive a gift that is damaged you must use your discretion whether or not you inform the sender. If it was insured by the Post Office then you can claim compensation, otherwise it will depend upon who sent it; unfortunately the giver will feel obliged to send a replacement, so you may feel that, on balance, you will say nothing. However, if they live close by and will visit your home then you will save a lot of embarrassment later by telling them at once.

Whatever you do, make sure you keep a list of who gave what as you open the gifts

The gifts are sometimes put on display at a home near the reception so that guests can go and see them if they wish. This is not always possible and it is not essential anyway. You can begin to write thank-you letters as the gifts arrive; it is not a task that has to be left until you return from your honeymoon. In fact you will be wise to make a start as soon as possible otherwise you may have an overwhelming task ahead of you. Whatever you do, make sure you keep a list of who gave what as you open the gifts. You should have written to everyone within a month of your wedding day at the very latest. Write to everyone, even if you have thanked them verbally, and never send out a duplicated 'thank you', that is discourtesy at its ultimate.

Planning your honeymoon

Whatever else you have to cut back on for your wedding, please do not cut out your honeymoon. After the rush and hassle of wedding preparations your honeymoon will not be just an optional extra, it is a necessity. We strongly advise against the suggestion that you just take a week off to work on your new house or flat. That is no way to begin your life together. Get away and have the best and most romantic honeymoon you can sensibly afford. As two penniless graduates we spent a weekend in pouring rain on the south coast of England and then a week with friends on an army camp! Hardly ideal, but infinitely better than not going away at all. We owe those friends a lot for making anything possible.

Try to get away for two weeks if you can. But we advise that you are not too adventurous; an epic journey across the Sahara is not the best way to spend a honeymoon, the purpose of which is to get to know each other as husband and wife in a relaxed atmosphere.

But even a honeymoon has to be paid for and prepared for. Make sure you have figured into your budget enough to cover the full costs, including spending money. Then be sure that your cases are packed well in advance and taken to a hidden destination out of the reach of your kind friends who have a fascination for opening honeymoon cases!

If you are travelling abroad and require injections then find this out well in advance and have the injections as far away from your wedding date as possible. Don't leave it to the last week and then find you are reacting to them! Better still, plan to go to some place where they don't offer malaria, typhoid and dysentery among the options.

If your honeymoon is abroad you will, of course, need a passport. Obvious it may be, but have you checked that yours is not out of date? Don't leave this to the last week or two. The Passport Office doesn't stir itself for weddings! The newly-wed girl can travel on a passport in her maiden name if she wishes, but in this case it is essential that you take your marriage certificate with you. On the other hand you can arrange beforehand for your passport to be issued in your married name. The Passport Office will do this, providing you ask for a 'P.D.2' ('Post-Dated Passport Facilities'). This is a small form which you hand to the officiating minister or superintendent registrar. He will sign half the form and return this half to you which you then enclose with your normal passport application. He will retain the other half for his records; he is obliged to inform the Passport Office if the marriage is postponed or cancelled. We suggest you do all this about three months before the wedding date. You cannot do it before the date of the wedding has been fixed.

Check and double-check your travel arrangements and make sure you have all necessary documents and tickets in your wallet safely. There is nothing worse than to start your honeymoon stranded at an airport having missed your flight because each of you thought the other had the documents. This is the husband's responsibility. Airlines and travel agents do make mistakes, so double-check all they give you, including flight times and numbers.

Often a couple will stay at an airport hotel for their first night and then fly out the next morning. This is to be commended for it saves any fear of missing a flight and you can start the next day in a leisurely way.

Don't forget to write to your parents when you are on your honeymoon. Just a card will do; they will greatly appreciate it. A quick telephone call, if this is possible, will give them a great thrill. Even if you don't want anyone to know where you are going, it is wise to leave your address in a sealed envelope so that you can be contacted in any emergency. When you return from your honeymoon give both parents a phone call as soon as you arrive back. You need not spend long talking with them, but don't let their first knowledge that you are home come from the friend who bumped into you in the high street yesterday afternoon!

The evening before your wedding

The week leading up to your wedding should be planned carefully and the tasks to be accomplished each day listed in your diary. Work out the week as if your wedding day was the day before it really is! You will now have one whole day spare. Although you will find plenty of things to do on this day, it should mean that your final day is not one mad rush. Plan the evening carefully. For the Christian couple there is a far better alternative to the 'stag party' of the world.

For the Christian couple there is a far better alternative to the 'stag party' of the world

You may have arranged for the final rehearsal at the church for the early evening. We recommend a rehearsal if this is possible, because it helps everyone in the bridal party to know just where they should be standing and what they should be doing; this eases tension on the wedding day.

In addition, why not plan a time of Christian fellowship for those closely involved. We always suggest this because it slows everyone down for a while and helps you all to readjust your sights. Set aside a time early in the evening when you invite all those closely involved in the wedding day to join you both at the home of one of the parents. This will include the Bride and Groom, the parents, the Best Man and Bridesmaids, the Ushers, perhaps the organist, and anyone else you would like to be with you. You may invite the minister to call in for a few minutes at a given time. Let everyone know what you will be doing so that those who are not Christians need not be embarrassed.

Spend just one hour together. If he is willing and able, the Best Man may like to take charge of this. First he will run through any last minute instructions for the Ushers, and check that everyone knows what they are doing. He can ask if anyone present has any query about any matter. This should not take more than twenty minutes. Then he could read a short passage of Scripture and lead a time of open prayer and praise. This is not the time for a sermon from an over-enthusiastic Best Man; it is a time for praise and thanksgiving. Within the hour he should bring it all to a close; perhaps arrangements will have been made for someone to bring coffee in on the hour. Then everyone can stay for a while to chat leisurely, but the Best Man should discourage people from staying on too late.

The Bride and Groom may want to spend a short while together. You may choose to go for a walk or a drive, or just relax for a while and then pray together before you separate in time for an early night. It is to be hoped that everyone leaves you alone and you are not bothered by people thinking of last minute things that should be done. Before you go to bed check that your clothes are ready for the morning!

If you are arranging the reception yourselves, it is all the more important that you plan to be finished well in advance and at least ask everyone to give you that last evening free of any duties. There is nothing worse than for a young couple to be running errands, washing plates, preparing food, laying tables, and joining the general panic with everyone else, and then to drop exhausted into bed at midnight or later. Plan to be prepared well in advance. What is not done, get others to do. If you have that fellowship time definitely booked, and a Best Man who is going to see that everyone gets there on time, you will all relax, worship, and fix your eyes upon the Lord who planned your marriage in the first place.

The morning of your wedding

It is becoming common for weddings to be arranged for the late morning so that there is not so much rush later in the day. In some ways the earlier your service, the better, because there will be less time to worry and remember things to do. Besides this, it is going to be a wonderful day so why not make it a long one? The Bride will have chosen her dress carefully, and at some cost, and it is good that she has the maximum amount of time to enjoy wearing it! However, whatever the time of your service, try to take the day slowly and calmly. Take your time getting up, and hopefully someone will prepare you a good breakfast. There is no reason why the Groom should not phone his Bride, unless he knows that she would prefer that he didn't. Just a few minutes, because she will be very busy.

Both Bride and Groom should begin to dress in good time. The Bride will have her mother or Chief Bridesmaid, or both, to help her, and she will need to allow at least three hours to prepare. It is wise to have a carefully timed plan for the morning so that there is no danger of running out of time. You may have your hairdresser arriving at some point and you need to be ready for her, already having had a relaxing bath; and if the photographer is coming to the house you will need to be ready at least an hour before the service. Those three hours will slip by very quickly.

The Bride is well-advised to have tried on her entire outfit at least a week prior to the day; this gives time to make adjustments and you will then approach your final dressing with confidence. A few words of advice regarding the Bride's head-dress. If you are wearing a veil, do spend time fixing it firmly in place; we have seen a number of brides who have gone through the service battling with a continually slipping head-dress and then discarding it in despair at the reception! Most veils come with a comb attached, but this is not sufficient; our advice is that you sew your veil to your head-dress, attach hat elastic to this, and with a number of clips fix it firmly in place. Cover the elastic and clips carefully with your hair. On the day you can then wash and set your hair and go confidently to the service and reception knowing that your head-dress is secure.

The Best Man should call for the Groom, so that he can check the Groom is properly dressed! He will then accompany him to the church about twenty minutes prior to the start of the service. The photographer, Authorised Person (or Registrar), and the minister, will all want some of those twenty minutes to discuss final details.

Brides ought not to be late! If the church uses an official Registrar, rather than its own Authorised Person, then he or she may well have another service to attend; if the Bride is late, the minister may have to shorten the service.

Now the time has arrived and we are sure you will have a wonderful day to begin your new life together. May God's intimate friendship bless your marriage and your home continually.

Assignment for chapter ten

Now we are three

This assignment should be completed **TOGETHER** *before you read the chapter*

1 Make three lists under the headings:
Our commitments, our leisure, our home.
For example: employment, hobbies, and housework.
When you have made your lists as full as you can, mark with a cross all those that will be affected when a baby arrives. Discuss how you will adjust with these activities.

2 Make a list of the particular responsibilities each of you will have in caring for and training your first child.

3 Discuss together any problems that you anticipate with grandparents. How do you propose dealing with these?

4 Can you think of any ways in which the arrival of a baby into your home could threaten your relationship together?

5 Finally, what do you both look forward to most of all when you are three?

Bible study for chapter ten

This Bible study should be completed TOGETHER *before you read the chapter*
Read together Matthew 18:1-11, and 19:13-15

1 What warnings and encouragements can you find in these verses?
Now turn to Deuteronomy 6:1-9

2 What does it mean in verse 2 by teaching our children to 'fear the LORD'? Do you think the answer lies in verse 2 and verse 5?

3 From verses 6-9 we are told how we are to train our children.
Make a list of the various ways in which this was done in Israel. Now write down a modern application for each.

Now we are three

HAVE YOU WORKED THROUGH THE ASSIGNMENT AND BIBLE STUDY?

A marriage can be happy and successful even if it is not possible for you to have children. We made this point in chapter six. Children may be important to your marriage, but they are not all-important. However, since children become part of most marriages, we have included this chapter.

You may be tempted to assume that during your engagement or the first year or so of marriage the subject of the arrival of your first child need not bother you. Nevertheless we encourage you to read on because not only will this chapter tell you of the joys and warn you of the disruptions of a baby, but, hopefully, it will also prepare you for them.

We must begin by stating the obvious: A happy marriage produces happy children. If you are still having a lot of problems and pressures, backbiting and battles, you must not think that children will solve your problems and draw you together; if you had difficulties before the baby arrives there will be double trouble after its arrival. On the other hand, if it has been all honeymoon since your wedding, that's great. But we should remind you that adding to your family means added responsibilities and less freedom.

Turn to the assignment and look at question 1. You may have answered something like this:

Commitments	**Leisure**	**Home**
employment	eating out	housework
finance	holidays	washing
church involvement	weekends away	shopping
social work	hobbies	gardening
	sports	car-cleaning/servicing
	meeting with friends	household DIY

You will have realised that everything on your lists will be affected one way or another. So, what happens when the baby arrives? The wife has to stop work which inevitably means less money; less money means less leisure pursuits; and less leisure means that everyday routine may become tedious. The husband complains: 'You are always looking after the baby' and the wife grumbles: 'We never go out; at least you can go off to work'.

Broken nights fray the nerves, and less finance coming in at a time when more finance is going out does not help. Pleasures have to change and eating out becomes an occasional home-delivered pizza; going to a good film or concert may mean hiring a video or switching to your favourite radio station. Instead of visiting friends for the evening there is still a pile of ironing to be done. Holidays are also affected; number three does not appreciate the adventures you once enjoyed, and funds may force you to stay close to home. Routine goes out of the window in the early months especially, as the young mother seems to spend all her day feeding and washing. And how on earth does prayer and Christian commitment fit in with all this?

But let's pick up on some of these problems.

Babies cost money

If you wait until you can afford to start a family, you probably never will. So you must discuss together how you will economise. Perhaps you will have to return to chapter four, because you will need to re-work your budget. All along you should have been planning for the wife to stop work. Babies are expensive and they grow very quickly which means continually changing to larger sizes of everything.

If you wait until you can afford to start a family, you probably never will

Most young mothers dream of having everything new for the first baby, thinking that this will last for future additions. However, on a tight budget you must not feel that everything has to be new. Have you heard of any baby suffering psychological stress because it did not have a gleaming new buggy to show off among its peer group? As the early stages pass so quickly, many items can be purchased in almost-new condition on the second and even third-hand markets. One advantage of belonging to a Christian church is that items are readily passed down, and no one should despise this.

Don't rush out and buy everything for your baby within the first three months of pregnancy! Something may go wrong, and anyway you will find gifts trickle in over the next six months. Save your money to buy the essentials that are still remaining at the end.

But a word of warning. Parents are often keen to give things for the new grandchild, but when they bring down from the loft the cot or pram *you* were reared in, you must stand firm and politely decline—unless, of course, you really like it. Fashions in prams and other items change greatly from one generation to the next. On the other hand, a sixties Silver Cross can be quite a head-turner among young mums!

Broken nights

This is the second thing that hits you. In some homes it takes as long as three nights for the exciting novelty of feeding and nappy changing at 2 am to wear off! From then on, the new father turns over grumbling: 'Can't you keep that thing quiet, I've got to go to work today'; whilst mother retaliates, as she pulls the pillow round both ears, 'You see to it; I have it all day'.

Although this is potentially explosive in your relationship, as a matter of fact both of you are right. So how did you plan to deal with it in your assignment question 2? It's true that the mother can occasionally rest during the day when the baby is asleep, but it is not fair that she has to keep all the night watches alone. Every husband should take his turn at midnight nappy-changing, so why not settle for a division of duties: if the baby is breast-fed then mother feeds whilst dad gains a few minutes extra sleep; then it's his turn to change the nappy and settle the baby. If baby has to be bottle-fed then a more equal 'taking turns' is possible.

It will not be long before almost every baby decides to have a 'crying time', and this is where the trouble really starts. There seems to be no apparent reason for this crying, and each baby chooses the occasion and the length to suit themselves. They just cry and cry—sometimes for hours on end. It can be very distressing for young parents, and extremely exhausting. But you must share it together. Don't panic, there is probably nothing seriously wrong with your baby apart from a large dose of 'the normals'. You will need patience and love, both for the baby and for each other until eventually your little gem decides enough is enough. You can be assured of this: all crying does come to an end—eventually! And if your baby decides to be better than all the others and follows the books in a perfect regularity of sleeping and waking, then just wait until they are teething. If there are still no problems, wait until number two arrives!

Where do I find the time?

Don't panic about housework either. Remember our Sarah Kay poster on the broom cupboard: 'My house is clean enough to be healthy and dirty enough to be happy'. The best advice we can give is **Be Tidy**. Find everything a home and return it there when used. A room that has every shelf and table scattered with magazines, papers and baby-bits, with books piled in the corner and almost every chair occupied with something or other, looks messy, untidy and dirty. So clear them all away and you will be surprised at how clean your house looks—and you haven't lifted a broom or duster!

When you were both at work the chores were done together, but now things will start to change because the new mother wants to show her husband how skilful and competent she is in her new role. To start with you will feel that you are feeding and washing all the time and that 'occasional rest during the day', referred to three paragraphs above seems a cruel joke! So meals need to be planned carefully and prepared while the baby is sleeping. You should be aiming to have all your housework completed before your husband comes home, so that, as far as baby allows, you will have an evening together.

There's no time for the church!

Every baby is a miracle. As the psalmist has said, 'You knit me together in my mother's womb' (Psalm 139:13 NIV). The marvel of conception and the miracle of a baby forming, growing and entering into this world as a miniature you, is breath-taking in its wonder. This so often brings a couple closer to God, as together you experience the joy and fulfilment of those nine months. So the arrival of a new baby into your family never *causes* a spiritual decline, it just highlights existing problems.

The writer to the Hebrews encourages us 'not to give up meeting together' (10:25 NIV). He does not make an exception when the baby arrives! We need the warmth of fellowship and the instruction of the ministry of the word of God to spur us on in our faith. If we let our attendance among the people of God slip away, we can slide into a gradual backsliding state without realising it. Your pattern of regular attendance at church for ministry and the prayer meeting should never be dictated by a baby. Not only is this pattern found clearly in Scripture (Acts 2:42 for example) but the patterns you set now will become part of your family life for years to come. If you get out of the habit of the prayer meeting when the first baby arrives, how will you hope to change when number two, or even three, comes into the family? Experience tells us that the longer you stay away from ministry and prayer, the more likely you are never to return. Remember what we said earlier: a new baby never causes a spiritual decline, it simply highlights an existing problem.

The arrival of a new baby never causes a spiritual decline, it just highlights existing problems

Here are a few excuses you will be tempted to use:

'The feeding-times clash with church'. This can happen, but no baby minds being fed thirty minutes or even an hour earlier to fit in with your plans, so don't use this as an excuse. Don't be beaten by the problems, solve them. To develop a family Sunday of worship, rest and the enjoyment of being together is one of the priceless gifts God has given us in the fourth commandment.

'Baby doesn't like the crèche'. Not many do to start with. Whatever you do, don't stay away from church just because your baby, or toddler, cries when you leave them on Sunday morning; if you do, your baby has won a decisive battle of

who is boss. Check out that the crèche helpers are happy to be responsible and will call you if things get too noisy; assure your baby that you will be back, give it a kiss—and go. Firmly and courageously. Most babies and toddlers stop crying within a few minutes of mum leaving and play happily until she returns—when they might start crying again! You can be sure that you will be called if the helpers believe the child is getting too upset. If you have real problems, work at it in co-operation with the crèche helpers by staying for a while and gradually shortening your time. If you give in now, what will you do when they don't want to go to Sunday School either—or day school for that matter?

'We get so tired with the baby'. If tiredness keeps you in-doors you will never go out again! Remember that an hour or two among the people of God does revive you.

'But she has had the baby all day and I didn't like to leave her'. Of course there may be the occasional day when baby has been so fretful and the young mother is so upset and exhausted that you will want to stay in together; in fact if she has had a particularly stressful day she should be encouraged to have a break and go out to the meeting. But your pattern should be to *alternate* on a Sunday evening and at the prayer meeting and Bible study.

'I don't like going out at night on my own'. This is sometimes the excuse of a young wife who doesn't really want to go. You can easily pair up and travel with someone close to you, or ask a friend to pick you up.

'But I don't know who to sit with'. This may reflect the danger that you have become too isolated as a couple. The church is a family, why not go and look for another wife on her own or someone you do not know very well. Besides, if you think like this, imagine what the visitor feels—so look out for visitors and sit with them.

What answers did you have for question 4 on your assignment? Here are a few suggestions of situations that will put pressure on your relationship. First for the mother and then for the father.

A word to a new mother

If you develop the right mind-set this can be one of the most exciting times in your life. If you allow the baby to dominate your life, it certainly will; but once you have survived the hectic first two or three months you can generally establish a routine that allows you a fair degree of freedom. Don't waste it. We appreciate that some babies are especially fretful or sickly but generally they are tough little things that will soon settle into your routine.

A new world of social contacts opens up. You can meet mothers at clinic, clubs, coffee mornings, shops, the park or leisure centres. What an opportunity to make friends for the sake of the gospel. Additionally, have you planned to use some of your new time to work in the life of the church? There are many areas of work in a healthy church that are open to willing hands. But beware that you do not become so involved in this enjoyable life that you neglect to maintain a home for your husband so that unnecessary demands are made on him as soon as he comes in.

Since you left work, the budget may be stretched to breaking point. We do not recommend that you return to full-time work and leave your new responsibility with a nanny, minder or crèche. God did not give you a child to hand over to a surrogate mother during its most tender and impressionable years. But you may like to turn back to chapter four and read again the up-dated version of Proverbs 31. Perhaps there is some form of home industry that you could take up; or team up with a few other young wives. Think about it.

★Don't throw a crying baby at your husband as soon as he walks into the house. If you think that the baby has been unreasonably demanding all day, remember that he has been working all day with or for people who have probably been just as demanding. He certainly doesn't want more demands put on him as he enters his home. Many young fathers want a little 'space' to unwind when they get home before they play with the children or bath the baby. Be sensitive to this and talk about it. It isn't necessarily a good thing for children to rush up to a hassled commuter as soon as he enters the home.

★ Don't greet him regularly with, 'It will have to be a take-away again tonight, I haven't had any time to cook'. This tells him what a bad organiser you are; there are many meals that can be cooked in the oven or slow-cooker. What you are really saying is, 'I haven't planned my day properly'. Or have you spent too long playing with the baby?

★ Don't grumble, 'I've been stuck within these four walls all day.' Snap! He may have been confined to an office, classroom or factory, and his time has not been his own; crammed into the steel tube of a rush-hour train, or boxed into a bumper-to-bumper crawl, wasn't exactly fun either. If he works outside, he may be longing for a day in!

★ Don't constantly complain that you are worn out and tired looking after the baby. We know that babies, housework and shopping are very exhausting duties, but planning your day is the key to all good management; you don't have to do everything in one day, and you can choose when to take a break. He may have been going with no let-up since he left home this morning.

★ Don't look dull and dowdy when he arrives home. During the day he may be surrounded by career girls who can afford to be a cut above the rest. Remember that you also are a career girl in top management, so make him pleased that he chose you. It only takes a few minutes to comb your hair and slip into something a little more presentable before he arrives home.

A word to a new father

In our modern world of commuter travel, a father is often denied the opportunity of sharing in the bedtime of his baby; this becomes even more acute as baby becomes a toddler. You will need to make up for this at the weekend and spend as much time as you can with your young family. To this end you may well have to forgo some or all of your hobby or sporting time. Your baby and your wife have a right to your time. That is your new priority. Settle it now that when a baby arrives you no longer have a right to so much time on the golf course, football pitch or the river bank. If you disagree, please don't get married.

In spite of all we have said about the exciting new world for a young mother at home with her baby, don't forget that this can at times be an exhausting experience. When a baby is teething or unwell, it is the mother who takes the full weight and burden of caring; to listen to your child crying for hours on end, or sobbing with pain, or simply fretful all day, is very tiring. Try to understand how she feels when you come home in a bad mood after a frustrating day at work.

Here are a few don'ts for you as well.

★ Don't take your wife for granted. She still wants to be noticed and appreciated when you walk through the door.

★ Don't go straight to the baby and show it your affection and attention when you come home. Why not? For the reason that we have just given.

★ Don't assume that you alone have the right to spend the evening relaxing. She too would like some free time; so, after the evening meal help clear away.

★ Don't be intolerant and grumpy when, on occasions the meal is not ready when you arrive home. The best planned day sometimes goes adrift.

★ Don't be too proud to pitch in with baby duties. In these days nobody thinks better of you if you are incapable of changing a nappy, preparing a bottle or bringing up the baby's wind!

★ Don't call your wife home from a meeting or a visit because you can't cope with the baby's crying. Your wife will be embarrassed at what other people think about your incompetence. Besides, when did she last call you home from work during the day for the same reason?

Jealousy?

Some husbands become jealous of the new baby because it demands so much of his wife's attention, time and affection. Of course it does, that is inevitable. When a husband finds himself thinking like this he must stop and realise he is probably behaving like a spoilt child; he must learn to share his home and wife with the new arrival. However, this jealousy may betray the much deeper problem that his marriage is not satisfying him.

On the other hand, a young mother must be sensitive to her husband. The novelty of a new baby may cause her to become so engrossed in smothering it with affection and attention that she neglects her husband. He comes home to a house in chaos, with no meal prepared, a pile of washing on the floor, dirty dishes in the sink and the place looking more like a doss-house than a home.

Remember that your children will grow up, find a partner whom they prefer to their parents, and then leave home. Husbands and wives are for keeps.

The solution to jealousy is to share the baby between you. There is nothing macho in the husband who boasts that he cannot change a nappy or is incompetent to baby-sit whilst his wife goes out for an evening. Duties as well as joys are to be shared. The more he is involved with the baby the less he will see it as a threat. The mother has a big responsibility in teaching a baby and young child to love and respect its father even though he is away from home all day and may have little time to play before bedtime. The way she talks about him and teaches the baby to say 'daddy' are all vital ingredients that avoid jealousy from the father.

Enjoy your baby

There are many joys to be shared when baby arrives. The first joy is holding your new-born baby in your arms and knowing that you have brought a new life into the world. There is also the joy for the mother of feeding her baby at the breast. But there is continual excitement over each development in your baby's life and growth. Make up your mind to enjoy each stage in your baby's development; nothing passes so quickly as babyhood. Keep as good a photographic record as you can afford.

There is continual excitement over each development in your baby's life and growth

Another great joy is bath time. We have a firm belief that babies should always go to bed happy. Begin sufficiently early in the evening to avoid rushing bed time. A child will feel insecure if you give the impression that you want it out of the way. So, a good playtime in a warm bath, lots of cuddles as you put on the night clothes, and as they grow older, a story. But always finish with a Bible reading and prayer before tucking them in and giving good-night kisses. This all helps a child to sleep securely. Whenever possible father should be included in this precious time; it is most definitely not just the preserve of mother. It is all too valuable to be left to one partner alone. Of course there are the exceptional times when circumstances demand a hurry, but so long as this is the exception and not the rule, then no harm is done.

Baby-rules or baby rules – OK?

'Experts' change their minds. At one time mothers are advised to feed baby at regular intervals, and then it is all demand feeding. First they tell you to make baby fit in with your plans, and then the advice is that everything must revolve around the baby. Bottle feeding was once all the fashion and then breast feeding came back. And so it goes on. The perennial problem of discipline is always up for review.

If you allow the baby to dominate the home, it certainly will. You should begin with the plan that this new arrival will fit into your family life with as few disruptions as possible. Of course there will have to be adjustments to times and routines, particularly in the first few months; but it is essential that you get a baby into a regular routine as soon as possible—and keep it there. Parents who allow babies to feed and sleep on demand will have children who are demanding. The baby does not rule your home—you do.

On the other hand, there are rules for the baby. Have you ever wondered why God created the pregnancy period in humans as long as nine months, and made babies totally dependant upon their parents for a period far longer than almost anything in the animal kingdom? The reasons are that parents need a period of time to adjust to the idea of an addition to the family, and once this incredibly complex addition has arrived, the parents need a long time to train and discipline the child. From the outset you must establish rules that cover every area of the baby's life. Either you have baby-rules or else baby rules. You choose.

We are not going to set out all the do's and don'ts for your baby, but you must talk through what is to be disciplined and what form the discipline will take. For example, when junior throws the breakfast bowl over the floor for the first time, what action will you take? Do you laugh, or is it a serious matter? God is giving you time now to get your act together whilst you can easily outwit the baby; it will not be long before baby will start to outwit you! Too few parents realise that many teenage problems start in infancy. Learn to handle discipline together now, and the problem will be greatly reduced in years to come.

Family prayers

Ever since the time of Christ, Christian parents have been teaching their children the good news of salvation. Humanly speaking, this is the main reason for the continued and steady growth of the Christian church world-wide. It was a pattern copied from the faithful Jewish household, as you saw from Deuteronomy 6 in your Bible Study assignment. So, you are now entering into a great ministry that has been unbroken for at least three and a half thousand years. It is your turn to pass on the gospel to the next generation.

The verses you read together from Matthew 18 and 19 are some of the most important you will find anywhere in the Bible on this subject of caring for children. Our Lord's strongest words of judgement (the millstone) are reserved for those who cause a child to sin, and his most rigorous demands of disciplined holiness (self mutilation is vivid picture language) is in the context of caring for children. Our Saviour taught that children are both valuable and vulnerable.

They are easy to mould and easy to mar. Whilst no doctrine of individual 'guardian angels' can be drawn from Matthew 18:10 (or from anywhere else in the Bible), this verse at the very least teaches us that angels have a special commission to care for children.

The Bible has much to say about the training of children. Go back to your Bible study for this chapter and questions 2 and 3. You will have discovered that fearing the Lord has a two-fold fulfilment: obedience and love. But did you see that verses 5 and 6 begin with you as parents? Only when we are living a consistent Christian life will we be able to impress the gospel on our children.

Surely your desire for your home will be that of Job who, you may recall from chapter two, could look back to the time, 'When God's intimate friendship blessed my house, when the Almighty was still with me and my children were around me' (Job 29:4-5 NIV). The intimate friendship of God with any family starts with the family at prayer.

Babies should breathe the atmosphere of a prayerful home

If you have been following a regular pattern of family prayers as we recommended in chapter two, you will not need us to encourage you to continue. But perhaps things have slipped recently. Now is the best time to start again. If you leave it any longer it is likely to disappear from your life for ever. Nothing is more important than that your new baby should grow up never remembering a time when it did not pray with its parents. Babies should breathe the atmosphere of a prayerful home.

Choose a time in the day when you can all be together, perhaps at a meal or before bed-time. The length of time is not important, providing it is not too long! But it must be regular. From the first day you bring baby home from hospital pray with your child.

In the early months of family prayers you cannot expect a devoutly attentive child! It doesn't really matter if baby is asleep, or even crying, or playing in the high-chair; slowly you will notice that there is a recognition of what grace and prayers are. It is exciting to see the first occasion when a baby puts its hands together or gabbles its own grace.

This consistent Christian life also refers to church attendance. Praying daily with your baby and yet not worshipping together as a family is inconsistent. A child needs to learn the importance of worshipping together, so you must get to church as a family for the morning service. Of course this may upset your plans, but remember your task is to train, and you will soon work out a Sunday routine.

You may have difficulties with crèche facilities in your church. If there isn't one you may have to start one! But talk over any problems with your church leaders, because it is important that your child knows, and is known by, the church family. A child observes and understands much earlier than many parents realise. So be consistent.

The importance of grandparents

You can't avoid them, and you wouldn't have a baby without them! They can be extremely useful at times, and infuriating at other times. You love them when they are willing to baby-sit, and can well do without them when they are interfering.

Start right. Don't be so protective of your new baby that you are afraid to invite the grandparents to hold it on their first visit. Remember that they have both held a baby in their arms before. That invitation to cuddle the new arrival will do wonders for family relationships.

There are many potential areas of tension with grandparents, but in every case you must talk over the problem together and decide which of you is the best one to speak to the grandparents involved. By now you should have learnt how to talk rather than fight and you must avoid all those accusations at each other's parents. Your assignment question 3 will have alerted you to some potential conflicts.

Try to be even-handed in your visits to grandparents. This is not simple when one or both live at a distance from you, but make sure that visiting your parents does not become a point of disagreement in your own home.

Be patient with grandparents who never cease offering advice on how to bring up your family; remember that they intend to be helpful and they will have some wisdom to share. If it becomes all too much, don't turn it into an argument, but decide which of you will courteously remind them that some things have changed over the years and that you must be allowed to bring up the family in your own way. Generally grandparents will get the message if you make the point tactfully.

If one parent smothers your baby with lavish gifts, whether they can afford it or not, it is likely to create bad feeling between the families; more importantly it spells disaster later on when the child grows up and learns which grandparent is worth adopting as favourite. Watch for any sign of favouritism and firmly check it early on. You can easily explain that you do not want your child to grow up having everything on demand; some things are worth waiting for, and you would rather be in control of what presents are bought at each stage of your child's development. It is never wise for grandparents always to bring 'a little gift for the children' whenever they call. You can tactfully explain that as the children grow up they will come to expect a gift from grandma on each visit, and that you want them to love grandma and granddad for their own sake, and not for the sake of presents and treats.

Don't over-use grandparents for baby-sitting and therefore give the impression that this is their only value. If you can develop and keep an enjoyable relationship with grandparents, which means not becoming so involved that they are for ever in your home doting on the baby, then grandparents can be great fun and an immense help. Work together to build this relationship, and deal with problems as soon as they arise.

Babies are for ever

What answers have you for the last question on your assignment? Perhaps you thought of the joy of bringing another life into this world; as you watch the development of your baby, the miracle will appear to grow. There are a thousand special joys: the cuddles and kisses, the first smile and faltering steps, and the admiring onlookers. Then comes the tears of training teenagers! By the way, one reason why we recommend that you do not wait too long before starting a family, is that you ideally want to be young enough to enjoy your teenager's life as well.

when a baby comes into your family you have taken on a great privilege and an enormous responsibility

So, when a baby comes into your family you have taken on a great privilege and an enormous responsibility. Although you are not responsible for the rest of your child's life, and there will come a time when you must allow it to fly from the nest and make its own way in the world, yet you will never again be able to live as if that child had not come into your home. What is more, you have had the joy and privilege of starting it off in the right direction, giving it the love and care that it needs, and of laying such a foundation that, prayerfully, will bring your child into a true faith in Christ as Saviour and Lord.

Assignment for chapter eleven

One Year On

For those who started **No Longer Two** *at the beginning and worked their way through, this chapter is intended as a twelve month review. We would discourage you from reading this chapter before the first year of your marriage has passed. If you used this book when you were already well into your marriage, you should still allow twelve months to pass before reading this final chapter. There is certainly nothing to be gained by tackling the assignments or the chapter in isolation from the first seven chapters.*

Please complete this assignment on your own and without reference to your partner. Find some unhurried time because you will need to think through your responses carefully. Discuss it together only as you read the chapter.

1 As you look back over the past twelve months have you found communication together enjoyable or difficult?

2 Is there a clear leader in your partnership, and if so, who is it? Are you both happy with this?

3 On average how often each week have you had 'family prayers'? Are you satisfied with this and have they been meaningful occasions?

4 Are you both happy with your relationship with the respective in-laws?

5 Are you comfortable with the way you are both managing your finances?

6 Is there any area of responsibility that has led to friction between you? If so, how have you tried to resolve it?

7 Have you ever thought to yourself, 'If only I had known that before we got married…'? If so, have you been able to talk together about the problem?

8 What single issue has presented you both with the biggest problem over the past twelve months? How do you think you have both handled it? Successfully—unsuccessfully.

9 In what areas do you think that you have not offered your best as a husband/wife?

10 What do you believe you personally have specifically done to make your first year a success?

11 How regularly have you reserved an evening each week just to be together?

12 Do you think you have both grown in your love for Christ and in your understanding of the Christian faith over the past twelve months?

13 After one year of marriage, are you enthusiastic and excited about the next fifty or more years that may lie ahead of you?

Bible study for chapter eleven

You should complete this study TOGETHER *before you read the chapter.*
Read Philippians 2:1-11

This is a magnificent passage to describe the humility of Christ, but its purpose is to remind Christians what their own relationship together should be like.

1 What are the five words Paul uses in verse 1 to describe good Christian relationships? To what extent have you experienced each of these in your relationship together over the past twelve months?

2 What distinct aspect of our relationship is Paul referring to in each of verses 2-4? Try to sum up each verse in one word.

3 Discuss together some areas where you each feel that the other partner has fulfilled these verses.

4 Talk through the self sacrificing humility of Christ described in verses 6-8. Can you see how this applies to your relationship together?

5 Verses 9-11 refer to the Father's response to this. He will ensure that Christ is honoured. What would be the best evidence in your marriage that you each had the same attitude as Christ himself?

One Year On

Please do not read this chapter within twelve months of completing the first seven chapters and not before you have completed the assignment and Bible Study either. Set aside an unhurried evening to read and talk over this chapter together. If you had two wise friends to help you when you first studied this book, you may want to invite them to join you for an evening of discussion. They should read this chapter first and perhaps lead the evening in order to draw from you both the issues that need discussing.

Congratulations on the first anniversary of either your wedding day or the time you completed the first chapters of this book. If you haven't yet reached that anniversary then you are clearly cheating! So why is this chapter intended to be kept for one year on? Because you set out a year ago with great expectations and high hopes of success. A thousand issues have arisen since then, some of which were potential threats to the security of your marriage.

At this point we suggest that you go through your assignments together to discover any unresolved problems. These will be located where one of you may give a positive answer at a point where the other partner is negative. Try to come to an agreement on where the real issues lie; you need not resolve them immediately, the first step is to identify them. But you must not ignore them or bury them either.

Looking back

It is possible that you can both honestly say this past year has been the best year of your lives. Your steady growing into a shared life together, the enjoyment you have experienced in home-making, entertaining, Christian service, and just being together, and the pride you have in your partner, have all deepened your love and enriched your experience; perhaps everything from the kitchen to the bedroom has exceeded your expectation in its joy and fulfilment. All this is possible.

On the other hand, as you filled in your assignment, perhaps there were some bad crises that came flooding into your mind. Disagreements that neither of you handled particularly well, situations that you think are best forgotten, clashes of temperament or annoying habits that are still niggling away at your marriage, and things said that you wish could be un-said. Don't despair. Your first year may have been more normal than you imagine!

Perhaps you have forgotten that a year ago we warned, 'A happy marriage

comes from hard work. It doesn't come from books, magazines or stories; least of all from television programmes or dreams and wishful thinking or sweet words on the settee'. Someone has called marriage, 'A total commitment of the total person for the total life'. You are now realising what 'total commitment' means! We also reminded you of Charles Swindoll's description of marriage:
It takes longer than you planned
It costs more than you expected
It is messier than you anticipated
It requires greater determination than you thought

So, don't be discouraged if this has been the toughest year of your life and either or both of you feel a sense of 'let down'. The first twelve months of many marriages are difficult months and we would go further, and unhesitatingly say that the first twelve months in ***every*** marriage should not be the best. Think about that together. However brilliant your relationship has been so far, it will be a tragedy if you've nothing better to look forward to. If you have really enjoyed your first twelve months you must still work hard for the future. Every anniversary you should check that your love for each other has deepened and that your marriage has matured.

If you have really enjoyed your first twelve months you must still work hard for the future

For your encouragement we have known couples whose marriage nearly fell apart after one or a few years, but who are models of a happy home today. What turns problems into achievements?

★ Are you determined to make ***your*** marriage work?
★ Are you determined to make your marriage work ***well***?
★ Are you ready to be honest with each other?
★ Are you willing to apply the Bible to your personal lives and your marriage?

Looking back at anger

An honest approach to your assignment will have clearly identified the areas of tension. A seething anger over trivial habits or a simmering discontent with some of the deeper areas of your relationship will direct you to the chapters in this book that you need to work through again together.

Perhaps one or both of you have not really accepted the differences between you nor the distinctive husband and wife relationship taught in the Bible; or perhaps you have neglected regular family prayers, and whilst one partner longs to re-establish them, the other seems disinterested. Then set aside time to read again chapter two and work through the Bible Study for that chapter.

If the problem revolves around in-laws or other relatives and they have caused more friction between you than you imagined was possible, then work through chapter three again. Maybe you have constantly argued over your individual roles in the home; in this case focus on chapter four. If finance seems to have got out of control, then chapter five is essential re-reading for you.

Very likely you have discovered areas of annoying trivialities, or significant tornadoes that you have not handled well and you are simply getting on each other's nerves. Chapter six needs your urgent re-attention.

Sadly your tensions may have arisen from problems where you anticipated so much happiness, and your intimate life of love has been an area of disappointment. We did warn that there could be difficulty here, but it will never be anything that cannot be overcome. Go through chapter seven together, and if it does not deal with your particular area of difficulty then seek the help of a counsellor. We have talked with couples who, years after their wedding day, have admitted they had a disastrous first night which left one embarrassed and the other frustrated. Because they had not talked about it together, it had affected their close relationship for many years. You may have had a similar experience during the past year. Don't worry, but at the right time you must discuss the problems and assure each other of your love. Whatever you do, don't just ignore problems; they don't go away, they just grow.

Number three may already be with you, or on the way, and that may not have been planned. Chapter ten ought to be read now, and if necessary, re-read. But above all, enjoy the preparation for and arrival of the new baby. However 'inconvenient' the timing or 'unplanned' the event remember:

★ That is no fault of your baby.
★ It is ***your*** baby—together.
★ Every baby is an exciting event.
★ There are no 'accidents' with God.

Whatever area of your relationship may be causing tension or anger, it can certainly be resolved providing you are willing to be honest and talk together, and each of you is ready to apply biblical principles.

Any cause of anger in your marriage must be resolved, not simply identified. One of the most dangerous types of fire is that which smoulders. There are no flames and there may be little smoke, so no-one can see the creeping fire until the whole room explodes into flame. Repressed but unresolved anger is a smouldering fire.

Change where change is due

Already you may be taking each other for granted or expecting your partner to change to fit your model of a wife or husband. Remember that it is not your task to make your partner agreeable to you but to make yourself agreeable to your partner. Our golden rule in marriage is that, *you aim to satisfy your partner rather than yourself, and in this you will find your greatest satisfaction.*

But some things must change. When you worked out your finances a year ago we suggested that within six months you would have to 're-negotiate the whole package'. Experience will have shown you where adjustments were necessary. Now is the time to re-negotiate on many areas of your marriage in the light of experience. The time you spend together, the hobbies or interests you follow, the division of responsibilities, or simply not allowing space in your togetherness. Are you pulling together or falling apart? You may need to work through the book again but don't despair. We know couples who have been married for many years who have benefited from working through this guide. No hurdle is too difficult to get over if you are determined to work together at making a happy marriage.

aim to satisfy your partner rather than yourself, and in this you will find your greatest satisfaction

Looking on the bright side

You will have noticed that the assignment does not focus exclusively on the problem areas of the past year. There has been so much to enjoy together in your relationship and this twelve month review provides an excellent opportunity to share what the good times have been for you. You may have responded positively to many of the assignment questions; in doing so you have shown just how successful your marriage has been in those areas at least. Build on these positives. You will be learning that there is no more secure place to be loved than in a marriage.

Sometimes a marriage goes so well that one or both partners take it all for granted. We forget to say thank-you and to express our gratitude to each other. The value of talking through your assignments together is that you will find yourselves sharing what you find best about your relationship; and it will provide another opportunity for meaningful communication. Not infrequently a marriage that begins with excellent communication runs dry. Busy lives and active Christian service can squeeze out communication. Remember, that just being together does not mean that you communicate together. Trees in a forest could hardly be closer together, but they don't communicate!

Do you recall the definition of communication in chapter one? We gave it as: *Successfully imparting your opinions, hopes and fears to your partner, and hearing and understanding theirs also.* One thing that may encourage you by now is the fact that during the past year you have talked together about many more subjects than you thought possible twelve months ago, and also that you have enjoyed the discussions. Perhaps already you have found yourselves thinking the same thoughts or anticipating each other's next move; that is the result of good communication. Whatever difficulties there may have been during the past year, don't spend all your time in this review focusing upon the negatives. If you have set aside a whole evening to review, decide in advance at what time you wish to finish with the negatives and start on the positives; otherwise you will both go to bed thinking that the year has been an unqualified disaster, and wondering whether your partner regrets having married you. That is not the best way to end your review!

Once you have positively identified the problem areas and discussed how you are going to resolve them, give yourselves adequate time to share together the best things about the past year. The events, experiences, things you have done or places you have been. Go through the Visitors Book and recall the evenings you have given hospitality; the fun and enjoyment and those hilarious occasions. But above all, talk together about what you have meant to each other and how valuable your marriage really is. Neither of you may be poetic or imaginative in the words you use, that doesn't matter. You will each understand what the other is saying. It is vital throughout your marriage that each of you should let your partner know, in whatever 'language' you both understand—both verbal and non-verbal, just how much you value them.

As long as life lasts

If you have been married just one year, you have only just begun. The best is yet to come. Whatever your future holds, look on it as the most exciting part of your life. However good the past, expect the future to be better.

This is not a vague idealism hanging hopes on unreality. We are convinced that for two people who believe in and serve the sovereign God who controls all events and plans all our lives, the future is always full of hope, confidence and meaning. As our own testimony in chapter one demonstrates, the circumstances of any marriage may change unexpectedly and drastically but that should not alter our love for each other or the deep enjoyment of our marriage.

You both made serious promises a year ago. Recall them now and reaffirm them to each other. Remember Ecclesiastes 5:5-6, 'It is better not to vow than to make a vow and not fulfil it... Do not protest "My vow was a mistake"' (NIV). There is a lot of practical advice in Ecclesiastes, you may like to study it together some time. For example turn to Ecclesiastes 7:13-14 'Consider what God has done; when times are good, be happy; but when times are bad, consider: God has made the one as well as the other.' Work hard at having a happy partnership marriage—and work even harder at encouraging each other during bad times. The benefits and privileges of this will be seen in your family and will accompany you into old age. A cord of three strands is not quickly broken (Ecclesiastes 4:12 NIV) so God will bless, keep and strengthen you both in this most precious relationship of husband and wife.

Also by Brian Edwards

The Ten Commandments for today

Brian H. Edwards

Large format paperback
288 pages £8.99

At a time when the nation's morality is in alarming decline, it is surprising that so little has been written on the Ten Commandments. Brian Edwards gives us a modern commentary, carefully uncovering their true meaning and incisively applying them to our contemporary society.

Reference: 10T
ISBN 0 902548 69 7

"Edwards' book finds a well deserved place at the cutting edge of application of this important theme."

The Banner of Truth Magazine